MONTEREY I..

LIFE IN A
CALIFORNIA
MISSION

THE JOURNALS OF
JEAN FRANÇOIS DE LA PÉROUSE

Introduction and Commentary by Malcolm Margolin
Illustrations by Linda Gonsalves Yamane

Heyday Books, Berkeley

9/03

ACKNOWLEDGMENTS

The text of this book owes an immense debt to Glenn Farris, who reviewed an older translation, correcting errors and suggesting improvements. The introduction owes much of its structure, thinking, and some of its best paragraphs to Roger W. Olmsted, who helped with the research in 1982. Randy Milliken was influential, not only for specific suggestions but for ten years of ongoing conversation and generous exchange of ideas. Tracey Broderick researched dozens of specific questions with skill and ingenuity. Rina Margolin did the major editing on the introduction and footnotes. Kit Duane made many fine suggestions, as did Linda Yamane. Dan Duane came in at the very end, fine tuning the language of the introduction, thereby sharpening the ideas as well. Others who helped either by answering questions in their field of expertise or providing editing, proofreading, or other publishing services include Elizabeth Weiss, Doris Sloan, Pam Peirce, Janine Baer, Norman Neuerburg, Stephen Bailey, Lee Jackson, Ed Castillo, Bob Brownell, David Ainley, and Larry Dawson. Special thanks are due the staff of the Bancroft Library, plus dozens of other people whose conversations, comments, writings, insights, and advice have gone into the creation of this book.

Copyright © 1989 by Malcolm Margolin
Illustrations copyright © 1989 by Linda Gonsalves Yamane

Interior design by Sarah Levin
Cover design by Design Site, designer Jack D. Myers
Typesetting by Archetype, Berkeley
Published by Heyday Books, P.O. Box 9145, Berkeley, CA 94709

ISBN: 0-930588-39-8
Printed in the United States of America
10 9 8 7 6 5

Cover illustration: Map from *Voyage de La Pérouse autour du Mônde*. Courtesy of Bancroft Library, Berkeley.

Originally published under the title *Monterey in 1786: the Journals of Jean François de La Pérouse*.

INTRODUCTION

At about three o'clock in the afternoon of September 14, 1786, two ships appeared out of the fog off the coast of Monterey. The handful of soldiers at the presidio and monks at the mission had been expecting them for some time, since news of their voyage had been forwarded from Mexico, along with instructions to afford them every hospitality.

The ships, *L'Astrolabe* and *La Boussole,* were French. Although San Diego had been founded seventeen years before, in 1769, and Monterey a year later, these were the first foreign vessels to visit Spain's California colonies. Aboard was a party of eminent scientists, navigators, cartographers, illustrators, and physicians. Cloth, tools, seeds, musical instruments, and other coveted trade goods were packed into the ships' holds. But more importantly *L'Astrolabe* and *La Boussole* brought what this tiny outpost craved the most: news from abroad and the novelty of new European faces. Pedro Fages, governor of California, Fermín Lasuén, president of the California missions, and Estevan Martínez, commander of the two Spanish

3

ships also in port, all competed to see who could bring the most gifts and provide the greatest service to this distinguished party.

It is difficult today to realize how utterly isolated California was in 1786, or to appreciate the excitement that the arrival of these two French vessels must have created. Monterey was then at the northernmost extension of the Spanish Empire, some 2,000 miles from the colonial center of Mexico City, unthinkably distant from the cathedrals and courts of Europe. The presidio at Monterey and the mission at Carmel a few miles away were at that time two tiny clusters of badly made mud huts. To the west lay the restless waters of the Pacific Ocean, its shores only partly known; for the soldiers and monks who gazed daily toward its horizons its distances were enormous and daunting. The land to the east—the wide, swampy valley of the San Joaquin River, the peaks of the Sierra Nevada, and beyond—was still largely unexplored, its vast reaches inhabited by strange and likely hostile races. Only two fragile links connected the Monterey outpost to the known world: the thin, rough, north-south trail with the pretentious name, "El Camino Real," that went from Monterey to other distant, even more isolated and backward outposts, and the annual visit of the supply ship from San Blas, Mexico.

The arrival of the supply ship was the great event of the year. Goods were eagerly unloaded, items were counted, lingered over, and distributed. Frustration was expressed over missing requisitions, while surprises were gloated over. The soldiers celebrated, the monks held masses of thanksgiving, the wine flowed freely. When the supply boat left, silence once again fell over the outpost. The food, incense, candles, munitions, and other supplies would now be rationed to last out the year. A scrap of news or hint of rumor would be chewed over, discussed, and hoarded. As months passed, eyes would scan the horizon for the next ship. In years when it was late, the anxiety became almost intolerable, the isolation felt

4

with a horrible keenness. People saw themselves at the end of the world, cut off from even the most essential supplies and information. As Junipero Serra, first president of the California missions, wrote to his friend, Francisco Palou, then in Mexico:

> It is just a year last month since I received my last letter from Christian people, so your Reverence can well imagine how hungry we are for news. But for all that, I only desire, when occasion may permit, to know how it is with your Reverence and with my Companions, what may be the name of His Holiness, the reigning Pope, that we can mention him by name in the canon of the Mass, whether the canonizations of the blessed Joseph Cupertino and Serafin de Asculi have taken place, and if there are any others who have been beatified or canonized, in order to put them in the calendar and to say the prayers that pertain to them.

The monks and soldiers of Monterey were not alone in seeing the Pacific Ocean as vast, mysterious, and only partly explored. Daily conversation in the courts and drawing rooms of Europe included tales about the silk-clad mandarins of China, the whale-hunting Eskimos of Alaska, the grotesquely tattooed and utterly horrifying cannibals of the South Sea Islands, and other exotic peoples and places of the Pacific Rim. Such stories were based in part upon the reports of Captain James Cook's crew members after their return to England in October 1780, and interest intensified with the publication of the official account of Cook's third voyage four years later. The Pacific Ocean, it was now clear, offered wealth, adventure, and world-wide fame. There were undiscovered lands to be claimed for a monarch, unknown coastlines to be mapped, colonies to be established, and lucrative trade routes to be opened.

First, though, there were dozens of questions yet to be answered. Was Spain still a powerful presence in the Pacific Ocean; or, depleted by decades of European warfare, was it merely a shadow of its former self? Did the Manila galleons still make their annual runs laden with oriental treasures? How strong were the Spanish fortresses and missions in a land called California?

Other questions stimulated discussion. Would it be possible to open trade with the closed and xenophobic nations of Japan and Korea? In response to the Chinese demand for sea otter pelts, had the Russians extended their fur trading activities along the chain of Aleutian Islands into Alaska? Where else along the western coast of North America could sea otter be found?

It was with questions such as these in mind that King Louis XVI of France ordered the outfitting of *L'Astrolabe* and *La Boussole*. These ships were expected to spend four years at sea—exploring new lands, investigating trade possibilities, and reporting on the activities of other European powers—and no expense was spared in their preparation. The lavish outfitting of these ships was, in fact, a huge national effort, comparable in its great expenditure of money and investment of national pride with the space exploration programs of modern nations.

The most skillful map-makers of France collected maps of previous voyages, compiling data, comparing charts, and making corrections to create the most up-to-date set of maps in the world. Well-known engineers, artists, and scientists were recruited to leave their homes and families for the long, uncomfortable, and potentially dangerous voyage. Those selected included a gardener from the King's own garden who would be in charge of collecting useful plants; two astronomers, including one who was a member of the French Academy; a captain of the Corps of Engineers plus an assistant; a geologist; an ornithologist; two physicians and a surgeon; a botanist; and a number of other scientists, artists, and draftsmen.

Along with the volumes of maps, the ships' library was endowed with a generous selection of reference books. There were included the published accounts of previous voyages, natural histories, and books on astronomy, chemistry, and meteorology. There were floras, a book on the theory of winds, another on the theory of tides, and others on zoology, fishing, stones and crystals, the formation of mountains, the construction of thermometers, etc. In all, over a hundred titles were assembled and listed in the ship's catalog, plus "all the usual books on navigation."

The gardener, Mr. Collignon, was expected not only to collect plants, but also to introduce useful plants to others, and to this happy end was supplied with seeds, roots, and cuttings. His inventory included six bushels each of apple and pear kernels, plus many bushels more of seeds, stones, or pits of gooseberry, currant, grape, peach, apricot, plum, cherry, almond, melons of various kinds, artichoke, pepper, celery, chervil, several grains, and still other crops. A root cellar was created in the darkest part of the hold for the bushels of onion, turnip, carrot, radish, garlic, potato, parsnip, and beet roots. As the day of departure drew closer, longshoremen moved onto the decks of *La Boussole* a small forest of some fifty living trees and vines—Montmorency cherry trees, black heart cherry trees, white heart cherry trees, olive trees, quince trees, grape vines, fig trees, chestnut trees, lilac bushes, the "hundred-leaved rose-tree," etc. In addition, the gardener brought with him a huge assortment of trowels, knives, shovels, watering pots, tin boxes, mattocks, saws, and other pieces of equipment that he would need to tend, water, transplant, and collect more plants.

For the crew there was the most modern of foods and bedding, plus a considerable stock of spruce, malt, and other scurvy preventatives. But the most remarkable items of all are found in the list of goods and merchandise loaded into the two ships "for the purpose of barter and making presents." The variety, quantity, and expense of these goods is astounding. For months purchasing agents procured and dock workers packed into the holds articles such as 2,000 adzes and hatchets, 2,500 chisels and gouges, 700 hammers, 550 iron wedges, 1,000 pliers, 7,000 knives, 1,000 scissors and shears, 2,400 steel files, 500 pounds of brass wire, 9,000 fish hooks, 50,000 sewing needles, 1,000,000 pins, 600 mirrors, 1,800 glass goblets, 1,400 packets of colored glass beads, 1,000 steels for striking fire, 30,000 flints for the same purpose, 2,600 combs, 24 pairs of bellows, 4 large barrel organs, 52 dragoon helmets made of copper with plumes of feathers of assorted colors and kinds, artificial flowers, many kinds of jewelry, tinsel, ribbons, 1,200 ells of silk ribbons, silk and linen handkerchiefs, 50 woolen blankets, 80 quires of flowered paper, etc. And this is only a partial listing; the catalog of such goods runs to four-and-a-half pages.

In keeping with the magnitude of the preparations, the instructions prepared by Louis XVI and his advisors for this expedition are some 200 pages long and meticulously detailed. The route is laid out with the utmost precision:

> [The captain] will then cross the meridian of 105°, in the parallel of 38°, which he will keep to the longitude of 115°, endeavoring to find out a land said to have been discovered by the Spaniards in 1714, in the latitude of 38° between the meridians of 108° and 110°.
>
> After this search, he will make for the latitude of 27°5' in the meridian of 108° west, to proceed on this parallel in quest of Easter Island. . . .

There are instructions on where to land, what to look for, whom to meet, and what to bring back. Members of the crew are told how they should conduct themselves toward native people "so that

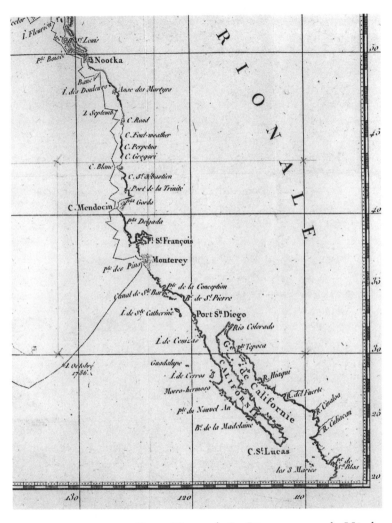

From *Voyage de La Pérouse autour du Mônde.*

the visit of the French, far from being a misfortune to these people, should on the contrary confer on them advantages of which they are destitute." There are lists of scientific experiments to perform and observations to make in physiology, astronomy, mineralogy, and other sciences. Nor is the study of what we might now call anthropology neglected, the physicians and other scientists being instructed, often in embarrassing detail, to observe "the passions, manners, and predominant character of every nation."

Of particular importance are instructions to visit virtually every point of European colonization and trade in the Pacific, to take navigational soundings, and to report on the extent and depth of other nations' colonization efforts and trade relationships. The instructions put special emphasis on the English occupation of Botany Bay in Australia and the Russian expansion into Alaska. They also request careful investigation of the presence of sea otters along the coast of North America, and a report on the status of the Spanish colonies there.

As might be imagined, the man selected to lead such an expedition was no ordinary person. Jean François Galaup de La Pérouse was born in 1741 near Albi in southern France. Born to minor nobility —he carried the title of count—he became a midshipman at the age of fifteen. Were he destitute of distinguishing merit, the rank of count alone would have been enough to secure him a comfortable if uneventful life as an officer in the French Navy. Yet from the beginning he displayed the qualities that were later to recommend him to the command of *L'Astrolabe* and *La Boussole*.

At the age of eighteen he faced his first battle, an engagement with the British fleet in the English Channel. Although he fought with distinction, France was defeated. (It was in this war, known in United States history as the French and Indian War, that the

French Navy was almost totally destroyed and France lost its colonies in Quebec, in the land east of the Mississippi, and in most of India.) La Pérouse was wounded, taken prisoner, and sent to England. Instead of enduring his captivity with sullen enmity, he took the opportunity to gain an understanding and appreciation of English ideas and institutions—an appreciation that stayed with him throughout the rest of his life.

After the war, La Pérouse was returned to France, and in subsequent years, while France slowly rebuilt its navy, he rose through the ranks to positions of increasing authority. In the late 1760s, he commanded various ships posted to the East India Station. In 1777 he was made first lieutenant, and by 1780, now in alliance with the United States in its War of Independence, he was once again engaging the British. In command of a fleet of three war ships, he entered Hudson Bay in 1782, destroying the English fortifications and taking the governor captive. It is typical of La Pérouse's breeding and character that after the military conquest of the British outposts, he left the survivors with generous supplies of food and ammunition with which to endure the rigors of winter.

La Pérouse returned to France a hero. Now 41 years old, he took up residence in the place of his birth, Albi, and married the woman to whom he had been many years engaged. He had already turned his attention to the affairs of livestock, orchards, vineyards, and fields, and was preparing for a family of his own, when he was summoned by an agent of Louis XVI and asked to head an expedition around the world.

He was chosen for his skills and experience, to be sure, but also for his personality. He was consummately tactful, kindly, witty, even-tempered—just the right man to trust on a mission that would require, among other things, the most advanced levels of diplomacy.

When we imagine the hazards of an eighteenth century voyage

around the world, we tend to think first of the dangers of uncharted passages, of storms, hidden reefs, scurvy, mutiny, shipwreck, and pirates. These were all very real. But more terrifying was the fear of unknown peoples. The explorers of the Pacific had to deal with cultures completely alien to Europeans. Cannibalism, unknown in eighteenth century Europe, was being recorded in gruesome detail by Pacific voyagers. Even the ancient nations of Asia were viewed with suspicion, and rumor circulated of the grisly fates of those who ventured to the shores of Japan or Korea.

In La Pérouse the virtues of the diplomat, the skilled seaman and the experienced military officer were combined. He was a man uniquely fitted for this job, and when King Louis XVI summoned him he did not refuse.

By late July, 1785, a crew had been assembled, the water barrels had been filled, and dock workers had jammed the last of the supplies into the holds of the two ships. On August 1st *La Boussole*, under the command of Captain de Langle—an old friend of La Pérouse's from the Hudson Bay campaign—and *L'Astrolabe* departed the French port of Brest. Their itinerary brought them around Cape Horn, with a stop at the town of Concepción in southern Chile. They then proceeded, as directed, to Easter Island and on to Hawaii. Although the King's instructions directed La Pérouse to sail from Hawaii straight to Monterey, the prevailing winds led him first to Alaska, where, south of Mount Elias, he discovered a bay which he named Port des Français. For the next three weeks scientists collected specimens of plant life, while La Pérouse traded with the natives for otter pelts. Shortly before he was ready to depart, a surveying excursion ran afoul of the treacherous currents of the bay. Twenty-one men were drowned when their longboats overturned in the heavy surf. Among those lost were six officers and La Pérouse's own nephew.

Desolate and grief-stricken, partly blaming himself for the disaster, La Pérouse waited three more weeks in the slim hope that a survivor would turn up. He then erected a monument to those lost and continued south to Monterey. His arrival at the Harbor provided him with a respite from misery. Here was a landscape not unlike that of southern France, and the men who greeted him upon his arrival were fellow Europeans.

It would not take long, however, for La Pérouse to discover that the men who came to greet him, and who for the next ten days would treat him with legendary Spanish hospitality, were themselves living in squalor. What we now regard as mission architecture, with its courtyards, gardens, and serene arcades, was nowhere in evidence in 1786; it would be several more years before Spain would authorize the funds to dispatch the skilled carpenters and other craftsmen needed to construct buildings with whitewashed adobe walls and red-tiled roofs.

The poverty of Spain's northernmost outposts was most vividly described by Captain George Vancouver, the British explorer, who visited San Francisco, Santa Clara, and Monterey in 1792. The settlements were lacking, in his eyes, any object to "indicate the most remote connection with any European or civilized nation." He found San Francisco's presidio to be a square "enclosed by a mud wall and resembling a pound for cattle. The commander's house, the largest in San Francisco, had a dirt floor "without being boarded, paved, or even reduced to an even surface: the roof was covered in with flags and rushes; the furniture consisted of a very sparing assortment of the meanest kind." The commander's wife, while "decently dressed," received him "seated crosslegged on a mat."

Vancouver found Monterey to be little different: "excepting that the buildings were smaller, the plan, architecture, and materials [were] exactly corresponding." The buildings attached to the presidio were "miserable mud huts," and the entire outpost presented "the same lonely uninteresting appearance" as San Francisco. This squalor and poverty, in the words of Vancouver, "ill accorded with the ideas we had conceived of the sumptuous manner in which the Spaniards live on this side of the globe."

The destitute condition of the mission and presidio should come as no surprise. In fact, it is far more surprising, in light of the outpost's history, that in 1786 the Spanish settlement had survived at all. The sixteen years since its founding had been exceptionally harsh. Crops failed repeatedly, supply ships from San Blas failed to come when needed, and the Indians proved deeply resistant to European ways.

Part of the difficulty, once again, lay in the isolation of the colony. Simply reaching Monterey was an undertaking of immense danger. A ship sent from San Blas, on a journey that is now a matter of three or four hours by airplane, might take two, three, or even four months if it ran into headwinds, and by the time it arrived a goodly number of crewmembers might be dead or utterly disabled from scurvy. Land expeditions took even longer and were fraught with even more dangers. The most famous of the early expeditions, the "Sacred Expedition" of 1769 which founded Monterey and "discovered" San Francisco Bay, provides a horrendous documentation of death, desertion, and shipwreck, as Portolá led his "small company of skeletons" north. It took them over a half year to travel from their San Diego base camp to San Francisco and back.

If merely traveling to northern California was such an epic undertaking, establishing an outpost and sustaining it over decades was a logistical feat of almost inconceivable difficulty. Consider, in outline, the magnitude of the task. Two monks and about eighteen soldiers would be sent off to this remote corner of the world—monks and soldiers, remember, not carpenters, farmers, fishermen, engineers, or others with practical skills. These twenty or so men would be expected to gather together several hundred Indians of various, often hostile, groups (people whose languages they didn't speak and whose customs they neither understood nor respected), draw them by whatever measures they could into the missions, and teach them to live by Spanish codes and morals. This colony was expected to cultivate European food plants in a climate ill-suited to their growth, dress in European clothing, and keep church holidays. In short, beginning with practically nothing, two monks and a handful of soldiers were expected to reproduce European civilization with the Indians of California as its citizenry.

Moreover, the aspect of European civilization they were trying to reproduce was not Spanish village life, which would have been difficult enough. Indeed, the behavior that the monks were demanding of their new subjects—chastity among the unmarried, long hours of prayer, obedience to superiors, etc.—was far in excess of what was expected of European villagers. As La Pérouse notes, "Sins which are left in Europe to Divine justice, are here punished by irons and stocks." In short, the handful of soldiers and monks expected the Indians to desert everything they knew about life and to adapt overnight to a most peculiar and highly evolved European institution, the monastery—an institution under which, even at the height of its popularity, only a small number of Europeans themselves ever chose to live.

Given such circumstances, it is little wonder that Spain's efforts in California produced so much frustration for the monks, misery for the Indians, and were—by almost any measurement—a complete disaster. The low point may have been reached in the winter of 1773–74, when Junipero Serra, founder of the California missions, returned from a trip to Mexico, and discovered that the crops at

Monterey had failed entirely. The monks, who had not had a crust of bread or a tortilla for thirty-seven days, were living on nothing but an unvarying gruel of milk and ground peas for three meals a day. The Indians had been released and sent to forage for game and fish. When the new governor, Fernando Rivera y Moncada, arrived at the presidio later that year, he found the soldiers lacking even the most essential articles. Some, he complained, had guns but no swords; some had swords but no guns; some had neither. And those who had guns did not necessarily have ammunition.

It seems, at least on the surface, that Spanish support for the California outposts was begrudging and inadequate. It had been, after all, nearly three centuries since Columbus first saw the Western Hemisphere, and three centuries is a long time for any country to maintain a zeal for expansion and conquest. Perhaps by 1786 Spain had grown too old and feeble—too entangled within its own history and bureaucracy, too beleaguered by other nations—to pursue colonization with any gusto.

Also, while California offered nothing in the way of gold or glory, the expenses of maintaining these outposts were extraordinary. To keep these tiny, remote, and unprofitable outposts supplied with foods and other goods, Spain had had to build a port at San Blas on the Pacific coast, complete with shipyard, warehouses, and a garrison. The port itself proved troublesome from the beginning. Food awaiting shipment rotted and people sickened in the tropical heat and humidity of San Blas. The harbor kept filling in with silt, and ships often ran aground. So expensive were shipments to California, that in calculating the budgets for the California settlements, the Spanish officials added a freight charge of 150 percent to the cost of goods, so that an item valued at ten pesos in Mexico would cost twenty-five pesos by the time it reached California. Added to these logistical difficulties was the fact that the various reports that reached Mexico from California were discouraging accounts of crop failures, Indian revolts, pleas for more supplies and foods, and interpersonal disputes between the missionaries and the soldiers. From the beginning Spain wavered in its resolve to maintain these annoying, costly, and (except for the number of souls "saved") rather unrewarding outposts.

It is clear that only one thing allowed for the survival and expansion of Spanish settlements in California, and that was the forceful, dominant presence of Junipero Serra. Founder and president of the California missions, he was relentless in his desire to expand the mission system. Looking into the mission records, he tallied the numbers of Indian souls he had saved by baptism, and he would fight with all his strength a governor or anyone else who dared hinder him from saving still more. Unafraid of suffering or death, even welcoming the possibility of martyrdom, his drive and his zeal served as an example to other monks who might have sunk under the depression of daily failure. Serra was a man who had been known to wear hair shirts, whip himself, beat upon his chest with a heavy stone, and hold burning candles to his body to humiliate the flesh and punish himself for his "unworthiness." He not only accepted the pains and discomforts of missionary life, but flourished under them.

Junipero Serra was a man of sharp features and short stature, only a bit more than five feet tall. With a body that was often wracked with pain, and a leg that was inflamed and ulcerated, he drove himself remorselessly from Mexico to California, from one mission to the next, exhorting, demanding, baptizing, and confirming. He neither ate well nor slept comfortably. His admirers praise him for the single-minded zeal with which he pursued the goals of the next world; his detractors can only wonder whether there were not internal demons from which he was fleeing with such desperation.

What made Serra so formidable was not just his unfaltering drive, but also his great powers of mind. Formerly a professor of theology in his native Majorca, his eloquence and learning, as well as his religious fervor, brought him favor with the religious and civil leaders of Mexico. He was not a man to be trifled with, and he would not gracefully tolerate anything or anyone that interfered with his plans to spread Catholicism throughout California. Had it not been for his presence here, one suspects that the mission system would have either disintegrated entirely or perhaps stagnated at one or two symbolic outposts. Instead, when La Pérouse put into Monterey in 1786, the missions of California while miserably poor, were still spreading along the coast. Nine had already been established and a tenth, that of Santa Barbara, was at the very time of his arrival being founded.

The man who stepped forth from Mission Carmel to greet La Pérouse was not, however, Junipero Serra. Serra had died two years before and lay buried at the mission.

The new president of the California missions, Fermín Lasuén, was then fifty years old. Born in Vitoria, Spain in 1736, he was of Basque descent; and although the letters he wrote seem to be in elegant and literary Spanish, Basque was his native tongue and he complained of an imperfect ability to speak Spanish. He took his vows at the age of fifteen, arrived in Mexico in 1760, and served in California from 1773 until his death in 1803.

Before assuming the presidency of the California missions, Lasuén seemed uneasy, at times even tormented, by his missionary role. His letters are full of complaints and constant requests that he be transferred out of California; or, if he were forced to remain, that he be allowed to serve as chaplain to the soldiers rather than as missionary to the Indians. Obedience, he claimed, rather than zeal, was all that kept him in California. As late as 1782 he wrote: "This land is for apostles only. I am already old and all my hair is gray, and though my years have brought this about, the heavy burden of my office has accelerated this condition greatly." He was forty-six at the time.

Despite early waverings, once he became president of the California missions Lasuén turned out to be, in the eyes of the church and later historians, a vigorous missionary and capable administrator. He would found nine new missions during his tenure, as many as Junipero Serra, and complete the chain of missions along the Camino Real from San Diego to San Francisco. Under his guidance the poverty-stricken wooden churches with thatched roofs would be replaced by the tile-roofed Spanish-style buildings, arcades, and courtyards that have come to characterize California mission architecture.

Early European visitors all seemed genuinely fond of Lasuén, describing him as an urbane, learned, sensitive, gracious, and introspective person. The historian Hubert Bancroft characterized him as "a frank, kind-hearted old man, who made friends of all he met." He was in many respects the opposite of Junipero Serra. Frances Guest, a historian and a Franciscan, compares the two early presidents of the California missions this way:

> Both were highly intelligent, yet Lasuén, gifted with a degree of perceptiveness to which Serra could not lay claim, easily surpassed him in human relations. . . . Both exhibited strong qualities of character, yet Lasuén suffered, for a time, from spiritual infirmities with which Serra did not have to contend. Serra was rugged, forceful, self-assertive. Lasuén was quiet, cautious, circumspect. Both were involved in con-

troversies between the military and religious, Serra much more so than Lasuén. And both defended the interests of the Church. But, in his encounters with the state, Lasuén was more adroit, more politic, more pacific than his predecessor in the presidency of the missions.

Lasuén died in 1803 and was buried at Mission Carmel next to Junipero Serra.

If Fermín Lasuén was urbane when he met other Europeans and diplomatic in his relations with civil authorities, his attitudes toward the Indians present another side to his character. In 1801, after he had been a missionary for over forty years, he would still describe Indians as people who, in their native state, are "without education, without government, religion, or respect for authority, and they shamelessly pursue without restraint whatever their brutal appetites suggest to them."

The picture that La Pérouse presents of the Indians, while differing greatly from that of Lasuén, is, if anything, even worse. A couple of days after his arrival at Monterey, La Pérouse paid a formal visit to Carmel Mission. In honor of his reception, the Indian neophytes were given an extra ration of food and were lined up to see him. La Pérouse's description of them is nightmarish: anonymous, lifeless, robbed of spirit, they seem to be a people traumatized, exhibiting what we would today characterize as psychotic levels of depression.

The mission records suggest that the people lined up to greet La Pérouse were those who had traditionally lived in the immediate area—the Rumsen (one of the main divisions of the Ohlone, or Costanoan, language group) who lived mostly along the coast, and another people who lived in the mountains to the south, the Esselen. The few descriptions of them from before the establishment of the mission suggest that they were a fairly handsome, dignified, gentle, lively people who lived in a land of great beauty and extraordinary abundance. Sebastián Vizcaíno, who explored Monterey Bay in 1603, characterized them as a "gentle and peaceable people, docile, generous, and friendly, of good stature, fair complexion, and the women possessed of pleasing countenance." A year before the founding of the mission, Miguel Costansó, an engineer with the Portolá Expedition of 1769, described the people and their landscape in idyllic terms:

> The natives of Monterey live in the hills, the nearest about one and a half leagues from the beach. They come down sometimes and go fishing in little rafts of reeds. It seems, however, that fishing does not furnish their chief means of subsistence, and they have recourse to it only when hunting has yielded little. Game is very plentiful in the mountains, especially antelopes and deer. These mountaineers are very numerous, extremely gentle and tractable. They never came to visit the Spaniards without bringing them a substantial present of game, which as a rule consisted of two or three deer or antelopes, which they offered without demanding or asking for anything in return. Their good disposition has given the missionary fathers well-founded hopes of speedily winning them over to the faith of Christ.

Modern scholarship suggests that for many thousands of years before the coming of Spaniards, successive waves of different people had entered the Monterey Bay area. Their varying histories of conquest and intermingling, followed by long periods of relative isolation, created a tribal and liguistic pattern of great complexity. No fewer than twelve autonomous political entities (often called "tribes" or "tribelets," for lack of a better word) lived within thirty miles of the site of Mission Carmel; five different languages (Esselen, Rumsen, Mutsun, Awaswas, and Chalon) were being spoken.

The Rumsen, to choose one example of many, were a group of about 400 people who lived on the southern shore of Monterey Bay and in the Carmel Valley. The name Rumsen has also come to stand for the language spoken by themselves and three neighboring independent tribal groups, although the southernmost Rumsen speakers of the Big Sur area had a dialect quite distinct from the northernmost. Altogether, perhaps 800 people spoke one or another dialect of Rumsen.

That so few as 800 people should speak a language and be further fragmented into tribal entities and dialect groups was impossible for the Spaniards to grasp. They were looking for Indian "nations" ruled by "kings"—or at least "tribes" ruled by "chiefs." And when the native population failed to fit into the European vocabulary and conceptions, the Spaniards concluded that the Indians had no government.

The linguistic, cultural, and political situation of California Indians has proven difficult for the modern mind as well. It is logical to assume, for example, that the various groups must have been isolated from each other to allow the development of so many different languages and dialects. Yet at the same time there is strong evidence of intermarriage, trade relationships, gift exchanges, intertribal ritual observances, and a host of other practices that indicate a high degree of intercommunication. The people of the Monterey Bay area seem to have been isolated and bound together simultaneously—categories which, to our way of thinking are mutually exclusive. But the simple fact is that our concepts of isolation and interconnection—along with other concepts of tribe, language, independence, etc.—which were developed to describe the realities of European people, are inadequate to describe the subtle, internalized, highly complex, and (to us) contradictory institutions and reciprocities that allowed diverse peoples to live in proximity for centuries without merger or conquest.

Not only did the people of the Monterey Bay area live together, but they seem to have prospered. Although in some years there may have been shortages of a particularly desirable food, there is little evidence in the mythology, the archaeological record, the reports of early visitors, or the handed-down memories of modern-day Indians that hunger was a problem before the coming of the Spaniards. On the contrary, the most common description of the Indians during the pre-conquest years shows them bringing gifts of deer, antelope, elk, and rabbit meat, plus fish, seed and nut cakes, and other foodstuffs to the Spaniards from their obviously abundant stores.

Virtually all early visitors were extravagant in their praise of the rich wildlife and resources of the Monterey Bay area. Each fall and winter steelhead trout and silver (or coho) salmon splashed up the larger streams to spawn in the clear, rocky riffles. Immense schools of smelt dashed themselves onto the beaches: Junipero Serra himself described one such school as running for twenty-three days, drawing Indians from the inland areas who camped along the beach and gathered the fish. Clams, mussels, abalone, and other shellfish were abundant along the shores. Great flocks of migrating geese and ducks—said, in those early days, to darken the sky with their numbers—settled each fall into the marshlands and estuaries of the bay. Deer were plentiful, as were elk, and herds of pronghorn antelope were said to run in herds of two and three hundred. Whales occasionally beached themselves on the shore and provided a winter's worth of meat and fat. Seals and even sea otters, more numerous and less fearful of people than they are today, would haul out on land where they could often be caught. There were also nuts—especially acorns and pine nuts, but others as well—plus wild roots and bulbs, the seeds of innumerable grasses and flowers, berries, and greens. In addition, the tastes of the Indians ran to foods generally avoided by Europeans—grasshoppers, groundsquirrels, mice, and small birds—that were often plentiful and relatively easy to catch.

Yet while food was plentiful, it was also highly seasonal. The salmon, steelhead, runs of smelt, migrating waterfowl, whales, as well as the nuts, bulbs, seeds, berries and greens each had relatively brief periods in which they would be available. Even animals such as antelope and elk tended to congregate in herds in certain places and at certain times of year, at other times being more spread out and isolated. To hunt or gather successfully meant that people had to be in close touch with the rhythms of nature. Timing was essential. Without it, people would not know when to prepare fishnets and head to the coast, when to travel to the upland meadows to gather seeds, when to store the nuts, burn the meadows, or gather tule to make their boats. Without timing, which for the Indians was largely encoded in ritual practices and observances, the people of the Monterey Bay area would have gone hungry, even in this land of "inexpressible fertility," as La Pérouse described it.

An appreciation of the complexities of Indian culture is difficult, even for those studying it today. Many people still characterize traditional Indian life as "primitive," those emotionally sympathetic to it often extolling its supposed "simplicity." The reasons for thinking this way are obvious. To raise a crop of wheat a European farmer has to plow, sow, weed, irrigate, control pests, and harvest, all with specialized tools, learned skills, and at great labor over an extended period of time. The Indian, on the other hand, is seen gathering acorns from an oak tree, taking what nature offers freely, all without apparent effort or advanced skill. Yet the use of acorns is anything but simple. It involves many hard-to-master and often elaborate technologies, such as making specialized baskets of varying shapes (some of them watertight), storing the acorns in specially constructed caches, drying, shelling, leaching, pounding, sifting, and cooking. To watch an Indian woman pound the kernels into a fine, silky flour, sift out the cruder particles with an elegant motion of the wrist, stir the rounded cooking rocks into the raw mix, and do the many other steps needed to make traditional acorn soup is to watch something of undeniable beauty and sophistication. In fact, if the entire process is measured carefully, it may take less work and certainly far less skill to create a loaf of wheat bread than a loaf of acorn bread.

Similarly, those who herd domesticated animals often envision hunting as a primitive activity, wherein the hunter goes into the woods, bags an animal, brings it home, throws it onto a fire, and eats it. What could be more "basic?" Yet the image of simplicity does not hold up under scrutiny. Deer hunting, to use one example, involved not only a high degree of skill, knowledge, and well-crafted tools, but it also entailed levels of religious and social complexity that we are only recently beginning to appreciate. The Indian hunter often underwent an extended period of preparation that included praying, sexual abstinence, dietary restrictions, dreaming, and other techniques to sharpen the mind, focus the body, and ready his spirit. And when the hunter was successful, he did not just throw the game onto a fire and gorge himself. In fact, in many cases the hunter would eat little, or even none, of the game he caught. A portion of the meat would generally be given to the headman of the village, who would put it aside for guests or others in need. Another portion would often be given to families and clans with whom the hunter had special ties. Hunting, in short, did not render a man "self-sufficient," but like other aspects of Indian life served to bind the hunter closer to others in strands of reciprocity. The continual, more-or-less ritualized sharing of food within a group gave everyone security; if the hunter died, was ill, or was down in his luck, he and his family would still eat. And beyond such practices among families and within the tribal group, there were complex trade relationships with those outside.

In short, individual Indians in the Monterey Bay area were not "self-sufficient." A man or woman left alone would probably die, not just from loneliness, but from starvation. The people of the area were bound together in a highly evolved web of economic and spiritual relationships, developed over millenia, that, along with knowledge of plants, animals, and the rhythms of nature, had sustained them in relative prosperity and security for countless generations.

If the Spaniards, and indeed most Europeans, missed the subtlety of the Indians' material culture, failing to grasp the degree of skill and social complexity in their gathering of food and other resources, how much more did they miss that part of the Indian experience for which there was little visual evidence—their political and religious life. The government of the Indians of the Monterey Bay area did not correspond even vaguely to the European forms, and neither did their religion.

Among tribal groups that consisted of a couple of hundred people, government did not entail the institutional structures or scale that the Spaniards had come to expect, not only from the European models but from what they had experienced with the Aztecs and the other nation-states of the Western Hemisphere. In the Monterey Bay area they found no palaces, courts, kings, constitutions, or standing armies with hierarchies of command. The "chief" (or "headman" or "captain," as he was variously called) was more like a banker, a negotiator, or an arbitrator than a king.

Political power lay embedded, not in a ruler, but in the more prestigious families, and decisions were reached by an elaborate system of consultations, negotiations, and consensus. The chief did not give orders; he arranged and, in the end, articulated the consensus.

Further, there were no generals, war chiefs, or warrior class to whom the Spaniards could relate. Although the people of the Monterey Bay area were constantly embroiled in intertribal conflict and skirmishes, they were nevertheless unwarlike. They had no specialized tools for war and none of the value structure that glorified war.

The native system of justice was also inscrutable to the Spaniards. Punishment was arranged by indirect and diplomatic discussions among people bound together by familial relationships and reciprocal economic and religious duties. In these small groups where no one was a stranger and where families felt responsible for crimes committed by their members, the judicial system bore no resemblance to the systems needed to regulate the larger nation-states of Europe and Mexico.

Because the Spaniards found all the native forms of government unrecognizable, they assumed that the Indians of the Monterey Bay area had "no government," but lived in anarchy. Likewise, the Spaniards concluded that the Indians had "no religion." They found, after all, no churches, no temples, no visible or professional priesthood. There were shamans, to be sure, but in truth these were more healers (or poisoners) than priests. There was nothing that the Spaniards could, or cared to, identify as religion. The sense that animals, plants, rocks, and all other things of the world were alive, powerful, intelligent, and possessed of mythic history in the same way as people; that the energy from the time of Creation still abided and could be sought; that Worldmaker (in the form of Eagle) had touched their land and bestowed power on the things around them; that dances and songs were to be performed at special times to put the world into harmony; that deer gave themselves over to hunters because of an ancient religious compact between people and animals; that dreams were real and provided pathways to the spirit world—these and countless other beliefs and practices, embedded in daily action and periodic ritual, the Spanish either failed to see, or if they did see them they dismissed them as superstitions or devil-worship. There was, in their eyes, only one true religion, the one the Spanish monks were bringing with them to the Monterey Bay area.

An obvious question presents itself: if traditional Indian life was so successful, if food was so plentiful, if people's skills were so advanced, if their knowledge was so profound, their political institutions so apt and their religious practices so fulfilling, what was it that drew the Indians to a mission run by people so alien and unsympathetic to their ways? They were not, as is sometimes suggested, rounded up by soldiers and taken to the mission like prisoners of war. Initially, at least, the Indians seem to have come to the missions voluntarily, even eagerly.

Part of what drew them was, of course, the dazzle of Spanish goods. Guns, metal, cloth, exotic foods, horses that obeyed people and bore them effortlessly and majestically for great distances, cows that patiently gave them milk, carts pulled by stately and well-muscled draft oxen, boats in full sail that came from beyond the ocean—these were, for a people who had never conceived of such things, bewildering in their power and beauty.

Even everyday items seemed wonderful beyond belief. These strangers possessed items of vivid red, for example—a color which in the Indian world, was of extraordinary rarity, found only on the scalps of woodpeckers and on fleeting spring wildflowers. Colored beads, to the Europeans a bauble of little worth, to the Indians were money, and they responded much the way modern Americans would respond if an alien race were to arrive in Monterey today and begin handing out hundred dollar bills. When the first native person courageous enough to approach the missionaries returned to his village with beads that instantly made him the wealthiest man in the area, others overcame their terror and rushed to the mission to ingratiate themselves with the monks and receive the blessing of instant wealth.

The influx of new goods and technologies brought dramatic change to tribal life. How mundane and dull the old style of money —clamshell beads—now appeared next to the brightly-colored trade beads of the visitors. The native stone axe looked shamefully inadequate next to a metal one; bows and arrows, no matter how skillfully crafted, seemed like children's toys next to the rifle. The prestigious families, whose prominence had perhaps always been secretly resented, now seemed laughably old-fashioned; how could their stores of feathered dance regalia, dried deer meat, and baskets of acorn even begin to compare with the bolts of colored cloth, paintings, metal items, and wonderful new foods of the strangers? Even the powers of the shaman over the animal world, once viewed as awesome, seemed paltry compared with the powers of people who could cultivate such an extraordinary alliance with the horse, cow, and ox.

As Indians began to look toward the strangers as the source of wealth, power, and prestige, the old balances, respect, and value systems within the native communities broke down. Whereas life in traditional tribal society had been relatively closed—those not born to the better families had difficulty attaining prestige and wealth—the missionaries offered what seemed to be an open door. Join us, they were saying, and you too can be *gente de razon,* people of knowledge; you too can worship our gods, learn our skills, possess our powers, and enjoy all the benefits of our way of life. In short, what drew the Indians into the mission was not terribly different from the forces that even today cause people to flee tight-knit communities and self-sufficient rural areas to settle in horrendous city slums: the dazzle of technology, the hope to share in the powers and wealth that are laid before them, a desire to escape a social situation that (once comparison is offered) many see as restrictive—in a word, opportunity.

The opportunity, however, had a price, one that at first seemed modest enough. To enjoy membership in this new community, the Indians were invited to partake in the ritual of baptism, thus allowing them to communicate with the spirits and gods who had given the newcomers such great power and wealth. What the Indians could not have understood, however, was that the waters of baptism were, in the eyes of those administering it, taking away not only something called "sin," but freedom as well. After baptism, the monks felt that they had an obligation and responsibility not to the Indian's body, but to the Indian's soul. The Indians had to be kept at the mission, by force if necessary, lest they revert to their old ways and stray into sin. To preserve the soul, the monks undertook to regulate the Indians' every activity, monitor their behavior, and teach them (by whatever means necessary) the correct mental and spiritual attitudes. The Indians became like students in a school, monks in a cloister, prisoners in a penitentiary; they were now wards of the church—their lives, their bodies, even their thoughts no longer their own.

Another questions presents itself: Why didn't the Indians revolt? How was it possible for some eighteen ill-equipped soldiers and a pair of unarmed monks to keep hundreds of Indians in virtual slavery for decades?

There were a number of factors. For one thing, the Indians had had no experience with organized warfare, nor did they have a tradition of war chiefs or strong leaders of any kind. Their non-authoritarian form of government, in which decisions were reached by long and often indirect discussion, protracted negotiation, and ultimate consensus—so appropriate for small, stable societies—proved totally inadequate for mounting a successful insurrection, which would call for military discipline and decisive leadership. To make matters worse, the Indians at the mission spoke a number of languages and belonged to several different tribal groups, some of them traditional enemies, so that it became even more difficult to launch a concerted action.

Also, soldiers with rifles and swords—a troop of professionals, trained in military arts, obedient to command, without wives or families to protect—are an especially powerful force, even in small numbers, against a people armed only with hunting tools and in-capable of large-scale organization.

The Spaniards also had an enormous psychological edge. They devalued the Indians' way of life—despised it would probably not be too strong a word—while the Indians seemed to have been burdened by the incapacitating belief that the Spaniards were power-ful magicians, deriving their powers not just from the bullets in their guns, but directly from the gods. Proof of the alliance between the Spaniards and the gods was everywhere: the monks were seen constantly talking directly to their gods, and it seemed obvious that their gods were answering them. To rebel against the monks and soldiers meant to rebel against their gods as well.

More incapacitating than the Spaniards' military superiority or their perceived religious powers, were the diseases the newcomers brought with them. Measles, mumps, smallpox, influenza, and syph-ilis—diseases against which the Indians had no immunity and for which they had no traditional cures—swept through the missions and spread in devastating epidemics to the still independent villages. The death rate was horrendous, and everyone—Indians and missionaries alike—was powerless in the face of it.

Today we know that in the absence of medicines, the way of preventing the spread of such diseases would have been through quarantine. But the Indians, who did not have any experience with the idea of "contagion," and who in fact had a quite different concept of illness, did exactly the wrong thing. Shamans, trying to locate the disease within the body, bent over the patient to magically suck it out and get rid of it. Family and friends, assuming that the patients needed all the support they could get, gathered closely around the sick to sing songs and lend their strength. Diseases spread uncontrollably, and the dying and their families fled to the missions in hope that the newly arrived wizards had the magic necessary to cure the new and dreadful diseases.

As sickness took its toll, other factors came into play. As has been pointed out, the image of the self-sufficient Indian is a false one. Without the complex of familial, tribal, and trade relationships, people could not survive. Thus, as villages were depleted by disease or flight, it became impossible for those left behind to continue in their old ways of living with a weakened network of support and reciprocity.

As villages were deserted and remnants of broken families settled into the missions, desirable territories become temporarily vacant, and other Indians living miles away now expanded into them. After a relatively brief time, the Indians at the missions could no longer return to their homes to live. Their land had been usurped, their patterns of economic sustenance shattered. Even the ritual calendar —in which was encoded the cycle of dances and ceremonies, the timing of the salmon runs, the ripening of the acorns, and the arrival of the migrating waterfowl—had been replaced by a European liturgical calendar based on a seven-day week with ceremonies keyed to events in the lives of European saints.

The severing of the Indians' linkage to the land was not just an accidental byproduct of missionary activity; it was consciously done, part of the missionary policy of "civilizing" the Indians. When Fermín Lasuén wrote about the difficulties of transforming "a savage race such as these into a society that is human, Christian, civil, and industrious," he concluded:

> This can be accomplished only by denaturalizing them. It is easy to see what an arduous task this is, for it requires them to act against nature. But it is being done successfully by means of patience and by unrelenting effort.

The unrelenting efforts of the missionaries produced virtually unrelenting misery for he Indians. Unable to rebel, their old way of life destroyed, they sank into the deepest gloom. The heavy depression that hung over Mission Carmel hung over other California missions as well, and La Pérouse was not alone in describing it. "I have never seen one laugh," wrote Louis Choris about the Indians of Mission Dolores in San Francisco. "They look as though they were interested in nothing."

"A deep melancholy always clouds their faces, and their eyes are constantly fixed upon the ground," wrote Otto von Kotzebue, also of Mission Dolores. Captain Vancouver likewise noted that, "all operations and functions both of body and mind appeared to be carried out with a mechanical, lifeless, careless indifference."

The missions of California were places of defeat and death—not only physical death, but cultural and spiritual death as well. This conclusion is unavoidable from reading what La Pérouse and others have said, and it is supported by what we can further deduce by reading carefully between the lines. La Pérouse mentions, for example, that the hair of the Indians was singed short. The cropping and singing of hair was not a customary fashion among the Indians, but used only as a sign of mourning. The fact that La Pérouse presents it as a general style suggests the prevalence of death, the fact that he was seeing an entire culture in mourning

La Pérouse also mentions that many children had hernias and were dying because of them. He points to this as an example of the low level of medical skill among the Spaniards who were unable to treat simple hernias successfully. But for us there is the larger question of what kind of overwork or other mistreatment of children there must have been at the missions to have produced so many hernias, an ailment which seems to have been relatively uncommon before the coming of the Spaniards.

Then, too, La Pérouse provides us with a shocking description of how the Indians were butchering a cow, eating the meat raw, and croaking like ravens with pleasure when they found fat. La Pérouse assumes that this was a typical example of the Indians' uncivilized manners, but that was hardly the case. In fact, traditionally people were expected to show restraint in all things, especially eating, and good manners demanded that one express little interest in the food that was offered. The scene of people falling upon a butchered cow and eating it raw suggests something akin to—if not starvation—at least severe malnourishment. Indeed, from La Pérouse's description of their general diet we might assume that the Indians at Mission Carmel were desperate for protein and fat.

The overwork, the hours of forced prayer (in Latin), the deadening of sensibilities and intelligence, the whippings, the remorseless tedium of daily routine, the utter hopelessness—all these things led La Pérouse, however reluctantly, to conclude that the mission resembled nothing so much as a slave plantation of Santo Domingo.

If we are to take La Pérouse at his word that the mission resembled a slave plantation, are we not also obliged to accept his judgement that the monks in charge were pious, austere, charitable men leading lives of great sacrifice and devotion? It would be easier if we could see them as ogres, bent on the destruction of the Indians, cynically using religion as a cover for their nefarious designs. The truth, however, seems more complex, and the real horror of mission life may have been that this "slave plantation" may have been administered by men who had come to California with the most kindly and idealistic of intentions.

It is as difficult to make generalizations about the missionaries as it is to make generalizations about the Indians. The monks were, of course, individuals, and although they all wore grey robes and had vowed obedience to the Franciscan order, they were of widely different character and temperament. Some were lovers of music, some were accomplished linguists, some scholars, some mystics. There were those who had saintly patience and almost complete forgiveness, others who displayed meanness and even sadism. The great differences between the driven Junipero Serra and the more irresolute Fermín Lasuén, discussed earlier, were part of a wide range of behavior among those we refer to simply as "missionaries."

Yet a few general statements might be made. Almost all the missionaries assigned to California had been born in Europe, and almost every one of them had decided to become a missionary before having seen an Indian. The missionary impulse, in other words, was not a response to real Indians, but to Indians as they existed in the European imagination.

What brought the missionaries to California was a product of church doctrine, monastic values, and the fantasies of young men in a cloister. Perhaps we can picture the mental state of a young monk deciding to leave Europe for the Americas. In the midst of long days of prayer, meditation, study, and yet more prayer, as he struggles against the weakness of his own flesh and the impurity of his own thoughts, his mind turns to the "poor heathen"—a race of people in a distant land who grew no crops, had no fixed homes, were ill-clothed, and worst of all dwelled in the darkness of spiritual ignorance, consigned (through no fault of their own) to everlasting damnation. These poor heathen were, in the minds of the monks who thought about them, "ignorant children" in need of a stern, kindly father to guide and instruct them. And many a monk, as he trod over the grey, worn stone floors of the European monasteries, fantasied that *he* would be that father. He would go forth, in the tradition of the ancient saints and martyrs, to convert the heathen of a distant land. The Americas offered to the prospective missionary an opportunity for renunciation and struggle, a battle not only against the weakness of his own flesh but a great adventure fighting the forces of darkness and evil in the world at large. In short, what brought the monks to California was much the same thing that has always drawn immigrants from Europe to the "New World"—an escape from restrictions and tedium and the hope of new opportunity and challenge, in other words, a fresh beginning. Instead of woods to clear, fields to plow, and crops to raise, however, the Franciscan missionaries came for souls to save.

Upon arriving at the port of Vera Cruz, the monk would generally be sent to Colegio San Fernando in Mexico City for training. After a number of courses in the various practical and theological aspects of missionary work, he would then be sent to California, where for the first time he would meet the objects of his missionary fantasies. In his letters he would describe the Indians much as he had imagined

them, "poor" and "childlike." They were self-evidently poor because, like the poor people of Europe, they dressed scantily, lived
in thatched dwellings, owned no fields, barns, or livestock, had no
gold or silver money, and were frequently "reduced" to hunting,
fishing, and—like *bestias*—even eating wild roots and berries. They
were also quite obviously childlike: their clothing did not necessarily
cover those parts of the body that adult clothing should cover, and
even the wisest among them were untutored in the various practical
skills, moral codes, and theological verities of the Europeans. So
it was that the missionaries set themselves up to be "fathers" to
these "children of nature," to instruct, to correct, to punish if
necessary, because like fathers they were responsible for the Indians'
behavior. Indeed, more importantly, they were responsible to God
for the Indians' souls.

If the Indians were ill-equipped to deal effectively with the
Spanish military and cultural dominance, the monks at Carmel were
equally ill-equipped to deal with the Indians. The European ways
of thinking and acting—so self-evidently superior in the minds of
the monks—made no sense at all to the Indians. Totally mystifying
and meaningless to them was a theology based on events in a distant
land, interpreted and institutionalized through nearly 1,800 years
of European church history, transmitted to a large extent in Latin.
The holy light that the missionaries tried to shed fell upon an
increasingly sullen, miserable people. As years passed and the missionaries had to cope each day with incurable diseases, passive
resistance, and a growing sense of their own failure, mission life
gradually went from difficult to horrendous, from inconvenient to
completely impossible.

The deep depression that gripped the Indians fell upon many
of the monks as well. Take, for example, the five monks who were
on hand to greet La Pérouse upon his arrival at Mission Carmel.

Foremost was Fermín Lasuén, president of the California missions, whose early wavering and attempts to escape mission duty have already been discussed. The other regular missionary assigned to Mission Carmel was Matías de Santa Catalina Noriega. Noriega arrived at the mission in 1781 to assist Junipero Serra and was in attendance when Serra died in 1784. A stern and apparently unhappy man, he seems to have vented his frustrations by an increasing use first of the whip, later of chains. In 1785 Governor Pedro Fages took the unusual step of bringing a formal accusation against him for having Indians beaten with chains for "insignificant" offenses. He returned to Mexico City in 1789 and was made a counselor at the Colegio San Fernando.

In addition to Lasuén and Noriega, there were three other Franciscans, all young men still in their twenties, who had arrived at Carmel the month before and were awaiting assignment to other missions in California. Francisco José Arroíta would spend the next ten years in the missions of Southern California. In 1796, still in his thirties, he was allowed to retire to Mexico City because he was "worn out by hardships."

Cristóbal Oramas would serve at Santa Barbara and other Southern California missions only until 1793, when Lasuén relieved him of duties because of "depression and hypochondria." He returned to Mexico City the next year.

Faustino Solá would serve only a few years, mostly in Northern California, before becoming "incapacitated for work by reason of insanity." He was sent back to Mexico City, and when he died in 1820 he was said to have been "out of his mind" for thirty years.

In trying to form a picture of daily life at the missions, the La Pérouse account provides us with some of our strongest, most often quoted, and most haunting images. But, one might ask, are these images accurate? Was La Pérouse a reliable witness? Does his testimony reflect what he actually saw? Before accepting him at his word, it is advisable that we examine the social circumstances in which he found himself, the biases he brought with him, and the constraints under which he wrote.

We can assume, with ample evidence, that the Spaniards who welcomed La Pérouse were doing everything in their power to impress and please him. He was the first foreign visitor to set foot on their shores. He was a fellow Catholic, a military hero, an ally of Spain in the recent wars against England, and the head of an important scientific expedition. He bore the title of "count" and carried himself with an aristocratic ease that could not have failed to impress the residents of this lonely frontier. The instructions that the outpost had received the previous year to welcome the expedition had come from the viceroy, and the letters of introduction that La Pérouse presented bore the royal seal. The men in French-style clothing who stepped off the longboats were accomplished artists and scholars, urbane and well-educated. The monks and soldiers watched as the scientists began jotting information into their notebooks and the artists set up their easels. The reports they were writing and the illustrations they were drawing would ultimately circulate throughout Europe.

We can assume that—like men everywhere—the missionaries and soldiers wanted the world to think well of them, and from the moment the ships arrived until their departure ten days later, would have done everything they could to present themselves in the best possible light. The mission and presidio grounds would have been tidied up, people would have been dressed in their finest clothes, the food would have been better prepared and the portions larger, the behavior of the Spaniards toward the Indians and toward each other would have been (to use one of their favorite words) "exemplary." We might assume that, without consciously lying, the behavior of the monks and soldiers at this distant outpost would have been similar to the behavior of such people anywhere during an "inspection," and what La Pérouse was witnessing during his visit was not ordinary life, but something a cut above it.

Also, La Pérouse was in basic sympathy with the missionary goals and predisposed to praise the missionary efforts. Like most Europeans of that time, he had no appreciation for traditional Indian ways. "The nature of [uncivilized] man is savage, deceitful, and malicious," he wrote elsewhere in his journals. For La Pérouse as much as for Fermín Lasuén, European civilization represented the highest form of contemporary human existence. The two men might have differed about the means by which conversion should take place—La Pérouse favored economic incentive, Lasuén favored discipline, dominance and the model of the church—yet both agreed that converting the Indians to European ways was not merely desirable, but indeed a moral necessity.

Beyond being temperamentally sympathetic toward the Spanish colony, La Pérouse had practical reasons to praise this outpost and to present its residents as favorably as possible. He was specifically charged by King Louis XVI's instructions to leave a good impression and make friends wherever he went. And on a personal level he clearly liked the men he met. He was touched by the generosity of the Spaniards, themselves so impoverished, who insisted on entertaining him as best they could and on loading his ships with great quantities of wood, cows, pigs, chickens, fresh vegetables, and whatever else they could afford. He was struck by the devotion of the monks and the loyalty of the soldiers, and as a fellow European he sympathized with them for the deprivations they suffered here at the furthest corner of the world. How, then, could he accept the friendship of these people, eat at their table, take their gifts, commiserate with their plight, and then betray them by exposing them to the contempt and ridicule of the world?

So the Spaniards lay before him the best that the outpost had to offer and La Pérouse praised what was good—the fertility of the soil, the plentiful wildlife, the generosity of the soldiers, the piety and self-sacrifice of the monks. When he criticized, he did so with obvious uneasiness, regret, and circumspection, with deep apology for having been forced to do so. His praise seems emotional and heart-felt, his criticisms reluctant and forced.

Yet it is this very reluctance, more than anything else, that has so disturbed recent apologists for the mission system. If the writer of these journals had been a Protestant, rabidly anti-Catholic, ill-tempered and sharp-tongued, with an axe to grind against the Spanish Empire, his criticisms could be more easily dismissed. But when a man of La Pérouse's sympathies, diplomatic obligations, and good breeding concluded, with such obvious and pained reluctance, that the mission resembled nothing so much as a slave plantation, the condemnation is strong, clear, and devastating.

Church historians, in an effort to discredit the information in these journals, have claimed that as a product of the French Enlightenment, La Pérouse brought with him a complex of ideas and anti-clerical sentiments that seriously biased his reports. There is, perhaps, a bit of justice to this accusation. That La Pérouse's opinions and prejudices are a product of the Enlightenment is obvious throughout the journal. He was concerned with the ideals of justice and social reform that had already led to the Declaration of Independence with its startling proclamation that "all men are created equal"—an idea that would very shortly lead to the French Revolution. He felt that a good life was possible on earth, not to be forfeited for the promise of heavenly reward. He believed in private property, a life of reason rather than faith, and, ten years after the publication of Adam Smith's *Wealth of Nations,* in free trade rather than the mercantile system of state monopoly practiced by Spain. He was an advocate of economic progress, and held to a view that humans—rather than being inherently evil, sinful, and brutish beings who must be coerced for their own good—were reasonable and intelligent, capable of appropriate action in their own behalf. He assumed that if the missionaries would forego the use of force, practicing instead persuasion, setting a good example, and offering economic incentives, the Indians would recognize the self-evident superiority of European ways and would quickly adopt them by emulation and self-interest.

There is, to be sure, a smug ethnocentric quality to La Pérouse's writings. The modern reader will be alternately amused and irritated by his self-confidence in the superiority of his own culture and the self-congratulatory air with which he enunciates the latest, most modern insights of Enlightenment thinking. His preconceived notions certainly prevented him from understanding the Indians with any depth, and the Church historians may be correct in noting that many of his value judgments about the missions are shaped by his Enlightenment philosophy. But, right or wrong, it is not his value judgments about either Indians or missionaries that stand out so dramatically and give these journals their impact and importance; it is his facts.

La Pérouse was sent to California to collect facts, and he was loyal to his charge. This was, after all, a scientific expedition, at an age when science was becoming increasingly self-conscious about itself and its need to separate data from interpretation. It had been barely a decade since Diderot completed his *Encyclopedia.* Twenty years before, Voltaire had published his *Philosophical Dictionary,* in which he advised that "Reason always consists of seeing things as they are." It was La Pérouse's attempt to collect encyclopedic data and to "see things as they are," not his philosophical asides, that gives these journals their power. We may very well question La Pérouse's opinion that free trade and economic incentives would have improved the lot of the Indians at Mission Carmel; it is difficult, however, to doubt the validity of his observations that Indians were being whipped, that they were badly fed, or that, dominated by the missionaries, they lived in a state of severe misery.

On September 22, crew members had finished filling the water barrels, loading on firewood, and taking aboard quantities of vegetables, chickens, and other foodstuffs, and *La Boussole* and *L'Astrolabe* set sail from Monterey. Throughout the fall they steered a westward course across the Pacific, reaching Macao on the south China coast shortly after New Year's day, 1787. Here a member of the expedition, Monsieur Dufresne, a naturalist, requested permission to disembark and board another ship that would take him directly to France. As he was leaving, La Pérouse thrust upon him a portion of his journals to take to France.

By mid-February the two ships reached Manila Bay, Philippines, and headed north. They sighted the island of Formosa, explored the Sea of Japan which separates Korea and Japan, edged along the coast of the Sea of Okhotsk (a part of the world then known as Tartary), and on September 5, almost exactly one year after arriving at Monterey Bay, they put in at a Russian Siberian port on the Kamchatka Peninsula. Here another member of the expedition, a young man named de Lessep, decided on an extraordinarily adventurous journey overland across Asiatic Russia. La Pérouse gave him his blessings, and also handed him a box of papers to be carried to France.

From Kamchatka the two ships headed south once more, crossing the equator and reaching Samoa in early December. Here, while taking on water, they were stopped by natives whose hostility may have been aroused in part by the crew members' sexual advances on their women. In the bloody battle that followed, several crew members, including Captain Langle, were killed.

Left short-handed by the attack, worn by a voyage that was now three years old, with signs of dreaded scurvy beginning to appear and with the sails virtually rotting on the masts, La Pérouse now set course for Botany Bay, Australia, where he found "a spectacle to which we had been altogether unaccustomed"—the sight of a British fleet anchored in the Bay. These ships, pendants flying, so welcome, so benign, in a word so "civilized" to the eyes of La Pérouse, had just delivered the first convicts to the island. La Pérouse entrusted still another packet of journals and papers to the commander of the British fleet.

He remained at Botany Bay for nearly two months, repairing the sails and allowing the men to rejuvenate their spirits. On March 10, 1788 he set sail once again. His schedule called for a final year of exploration and a triumphant return to France in June, 1789. He never did return, however, and nearly forty years would pass before Europe would learn what befell *La Boussole* and *L'Astrolabe* after their departure from Botany Bay.

By late 1789 those who awaited him in France began to fear the worst. Such was the prominence of his expedition and its hold on the public imagination, that La Pérouse was not forgotten even in the throes of the French Revolution. In 1790, with the *ancien régime* collapsing about it, the Soc..t, of Natural History requested help from the National Assembly with these words:

> For two years now France has in vain expected the return
> of M. de La Pérouse; and they, who are interested in his
> discoveries or personally concerned for him have not the

least knowledge of his fate. Alas! what they suspect is perhaps more dreadful than what he has experienced; perhaps he has escaped death only to suffer the torment of hope continually reviving, continually disappointed: perhaps he has been wrecked on some South Sea Island where he stretches forth his arms toward his country and vainly expects a deliverer.

Despite the grave concerns of this turbulent era, the National Assembly was not deaf to the plea. On February 9, 1791, while embroiled in efforts to abolish the economic privileges of the previous age and force the clergy to take an oath of allegiance to the new government, the National Assembly issued a decree alerting all ambassadors, residents, consuls, and agents in foreign countries to the disappearance of the ships. The decree also enjoined navigators of every nation to search after the boats. The National Assembly further appropriated money to outfit two search and rescue vessels which were dispatched from France.

On April 22 the National Assembly issued a second decree. La Pérouse would be kept on the navy rolls, his pay to be sent to his wife. Also, money would be set aside by the Assembly for the publication of those papers then in government possession. An editor was chosen to coordinate the material that had been trickling back to France from halfway around the world, and engravers were hired to make the plates necessary to reproduce the maps and illustrations. *Voyage de La Pérouse autour du Mônde* was published in 1797, with English translations and abridgements appearing quickly thereafter.

Speculation about the fate of La Pérouse and his ships continued for decades after his disappearance. By the end of the eighteenth century scores of plays, novels, ballads, and apocryphal romances had been written, sung, or performed. Rewards were posted for information, and rumors abounded that La Pérouse and his men were still alive somewhere in the South Seas.

Interest was still keen in 1826, when Peter Dillon, an Irish merchant, landed on the South Sea island of Tikopia, where he was offered in trade a sword hilt inscribed with the initials "J.F.G.P." Tracking down its origins, he soon found other remains from *La Boussole* and *L'Astrolabe*, and with the help of others eventually pieced together the story of the expedition's fate. It seems that the ships crashed on the reefs near the island of Vanikoro, among the Santa Cruz Islands, east of the Solomons. Natives of the island revealed that many had died in the crash—some said to have been eaten by sharks—but a remnant struggled ashore. Within the walls of a hastily built palisade, constructed to fend off attack, the survivors scavenged boards and nails from the wrecks and they built a frail, two-masted craft. Some of the men, it seems, stayed behind, eventually living among the natives, but they had died before the arrival of Dillon. The rest had sailed in the hand-made boat, never to be heard from again. The best conjecture is that they were heading for Manila when their boat came apart in storms and high seas. Whether La Pérouse died in the initial crash, whether he lingered behind on one of the islands, or whether he perished on the hand-made boat will never be known.

Spain's California outposts continued their slow but seemingly inexorable growth in the years after La Pérouse's visit. Under the administration of Fermín Lasuén and his successors, twelve new missions were established, bringing the total to twenty-one. Missions now stretched from San Diego to Sonoma County north of San Francisco. Over the years, the scatterings of mud huts with thatched roofs developed into white-washed adobe buildings with red tiles, large churches with stained-glass windows, enclosed gardens with peaceful and stately arches.

Yet despite their growing number and their architectural transformation, the missions of California never really achieved self-sufficiency, let alone prosperity. They were forever dependent upon detachments of soldiers to keep the Indians in order, and upon the yearly supply ship from San Blas to bring essential goods. When Mexico rebelled against Spanish rule in 1821, and in the mid-1830s issued the secularization decrees that took mission lands away from the church, the mission system collapsed. The Franciscans mostly returned to Mexico or Spain, while the few Indians who had survived a half-century of missionary activity generally dispersed. Some went to work as cowboys or domestics for the landowners, some lived as best they could on the fringes of pueblos, a few even returned to the old village sites or formed new native villages. Many were by this time Catholics and married into the Mexican community.

By and large deserted, the missions throughout California fell into disrepair. By Gold Rush times and in the years following they often came to be used as stables, warehouses, or even saloons. Many of them were picked over for building materials, as new settlers moved their wagons among them to plunder them for brick and tile.

As the nineteenth century progressed, Anglo settlers moved into California. With their overgrown gardens, crumbled walls, and outlines of stately arcades, the missions made compelling ruins. The newcomers found these ruins to be somber, romantic, and evocative. To people freshly arrived from New England, Kentucky, or Ohio, these adobe walls whispered tales of an age of bygone glories. The newcomers needed a history in this strange, new land, and as they looked upon the ruins they invented one. Combing through historic accounts, they selectively eliminated evidence they did not want to hear and plucked out of the historic record accounts that fed their fantasies. With little evidence beyond their own imagining and some carefully sifted "history," they created the myth of the missions in which peaceful, tonsored monks bestowed blessings upon the children of nature in an arcadian world of harmony and love.

In recent years, many of the missions have been restored, often with a high level of scholarly involvement. Many of the architectural and artistic details are amazingly exact, and much research has gone into making sure that the plants in the gardens are those that would have been found in mission times. The human details, however, are invariably omitted: the sight of men and women in irons, the sound of the whip, the misery of the Indians. Without acknowledging the pain and agony that were a major part of mission life, today's carefully restored missions do not portray history. Rather, in the manner of "theme parks," they use the ornaments of history to create a soothing world of fantasy.

More than anything else, La Pérouse viewed himself as a scientist, and he felt that the major value of his journals would be in the navigational and other technical information they conveyed. In a letter to a friend, he enjoined: "If my journal be published before my return, let the editing of it by no means be entrusted to a man of letters." The man of letters, he feared, would do the journals a fatal disservice by "rejecting all the nautical and astronomical details, endeavoring to make a pleasing romance."

Viewing the La Pérouse voyage the way he himself saw it—as a scientific expedition—we find it to be odd, touching, a bit naive perhaps, but at the same time quite familiar. Enthusiasm for science and scientific knowledge was boundless. No sooner had the longboats landed at Monterey and official papers and social pleasantries been exchanged, than the scientists set to work. Ornithologists ranged throughout the sun-dappled oak groves and meadows to shoot birds and later stuff them. Botanists, disappointed by the dry mid-September grasslands, nevertheless scoured the sand dunes and the margins of the creeks to collect specimens of unusual plants. Rollin, the physician, set himself up among the Indians to take measurements of their limbs, compiling tables in which he itemized and calculated the proportions between the lengths of the bones within their bodies. He also took descriptions of bodily hair and other intimacies that, despite (or perhaps because of) their air of scientific detachment, are today rather embarrassing to read. A linguist interviewed the Indians, preserving samples of their vocabularies and commenting on the grammatical structure of their languages. A geologist collected and classified stones, while others spread out along the beaches to collect sea shells and other examples of sea life.

This expedition was, in short, not unlike the multi-disciplinary expeditions that universities and nations launch to lesser known parts of the world even to this day. There is a distinctly modern quality to it, just as there is a distinctly modern quality to the writings of La Pérouse. The voice we hear in his journals is, if the grammar were modernized a bit and the word usage changed slightly, a rather contemporary voice. We are, after all—most of us, at least—heirs of the Enlightenment, and La Pérouse's urging of social reform, of economic development, of scientific inquiry, and his confidence in the superiority of western institutions are all familiar. If La Pérouse were alive today he would be right at home serving on the board of the World Bank or as head of the Peace Corps.

In truth, by 1786 the modern world—the world as we know it—had already begun. James Watt had invented the steam engine nearly twenty years before. The fly shuttle, the spinning jenny, and the power loom that would lead to the industrialization of textile production and the spread of factories in Europe and America were already in use. Along the east coast of the newly-formed United States, lawyers and politicians had worked out the final details of the Constitution that governs us to this day. The superficialities of clothing and style aside, La Pérouse was, in most of his attitudes and beliefs, a modern man.

If La Pérouse was a modern man, what about the missionaries and soldiers who greeted him on these distant shores? It is tempting to contrast them to La Pérouse and present them as representatives of Europe's medieval past. But that is not quite accurate. These monks and soldiers were, in many respects, educated men. The Franciscans had studied theology in Europe and taken courses in administration at Colegio San Fernando in Mexico City. Estevan Martínez of the Spanish navy had graduated from Colegio San Telmo, the navigators' college in Seville. Pedro Fages, the governor, had written a memoir that would later be published as a book. To read the letters of Fermín Lasuén is to read the work of a literate mind. Indeed, in the writings of all these men, one finds an intellectual and spiritual quality not too dissimilar to that of the people today who promote the sainthood of Junipero Serra and defend the mission system as having brought benefit to the Indians.

In short, mission life as it was described by La Pérouse did not take place in a distant country at a distant time among a people who no longer exist. It took place here, in California, and the people who partook in it were in many regards modern people. Two hundred years covers only three human lifetimes, not a very long period of time at all. And although technology has changed the world in many ways, it has not changed it as much as we would like to think. The events at Mission Carmel are not ancient history. They are, in fact, uncomfortably recent. And as we read the journals of La Pérouse, what we find unfolding before us is not a tale of a distant fantasy land, but the far more gripping story of our place, of our times, the story of "us."

The Journals of
Jean François de La Pérouse

At noon our longitude was 124° 52'. I could see no land, but at four o'clock we were enveloped in fog. We could not be far from shore, for several land birds flew around us, and we caught a gyrfalcon.[1]

The fog continued all night, and the next day at ten in the morning we perceived the land very foggy and very near us. It was impossible to make out what land it was. I approached within a league[2] of it, and saw the breakers very distinctly. Our soundings were twenty-five fathoms. But

---

[1] Most likely a peregrine falcon (*Falco peregrinus*).

[2] A *league* is three nautical miles, a nautical mile being 6,080 feet. Other nautical measurements used in the text include a *fathom*, originally the distance to which a man could stretch his arms, or about six feet, and a *cable*, which is a hundred fathoms or about 600 feet.

though I was certain of being in Monterey Bay, it was impossible to distinguish the Spanish settlement in such thick weather. At the approach of night I stood out to sea again, and at daybreak stretched in for the land, with a thick fog which did not disperse till noon.

I then stood along the shore at a very little distance, and at three o'clock in the afternoon we got sight of the fort of Monterey and of two three-masted vessels in the roadstead. The contrary winds obliged us to come to an anchor two leagues from shore, in forty-five fathoms, muddy bottom; the next day we anchored in twelve fathoms, within two cable lengths of the land. The commander of the two vessels, Don Estevan Martínez,[3] sent us pilots during the night, both he and the governor of the presidio having been apprised by the viceroy of Mexico of our expected arrival.

It is worthy of remark that during this long course, in the midst of the thickest fogs, the Astrolabe constantly sailed

---

[3] Estevan José Martínez was born in 1742 in Seville, and graduated from the city's famous navigator school, *Colegio de San Telmo*.

After serving as a pilot on ships between Mexico and South America, in 1773 he was assigned to San Blas, the supply depot for the new California missions. From his meeting with La Pérouse he learned of the Russian expansion in Alaska, and on his return to San Blas later that fall he reported it to authorities. He was then selected to lead important, and ultimately controversial, voyages to Nootka Sound in 1788 and again 1789 as part of Spain's last attempt to assert control in Alaska.

within hail of us, never being at a farther distance, till I ordered Captain de Langle[4] to reconnoitre the entrance of Monterey Bay. . . .

▣ ▣ ▣ ▣ ▣

Monterey Bay, bounded by Point Año Nuevo to the north and Cypress Point [Point of Pines] to the south, presents an opening of eight leagues in this direction, and nearly six in depth to the eastward, where the land is low and sandy. The sea rolls to the foot of the sand dunes which border the coast and produces a noise which we heard when more than a league distant. The lands to the north and south of this bay are elevated and covered with trees. Vessels intending to stop here must follow the southern shore. When they have doubled the Point of Pines, which projects to the north, the presidio appears in view, and they may drop anchor in ten fathoms of water, within and rather near to the point, which shelters them from the winds of the sea. The Spanish vessels which make a long stay at Monterey usually approach within one or two cable lengths of the shore and moor in six fathoms of water by making fast to an anchor, which

---

[4] De Langle, a captain in the French Navy, was commander of *l'Astrolabe*. He and La Pérouse were close friends, having served together in the 1782 attack on the British forts at Hudson Bay during the American Revolutionary War.

they bury in the sand on the beach. They have then nothing to fear from the south winds, which are sometimes strong, but not at all dangerous, as they blow from the coast. . . .

It is impossible to describe either the number of whales with which we were surrounded, or their familiarity.[5] They spouted every half minute within half a pistol shot of our frigates, and caused a most annoying stench. We were unacquainted with this property in the whale, but the inhabitants informed us that the water thrown out by them is impregnated with this offensive smell, which is perceived at a considerable distance. To the fishermen of Greenland or of Nantucket, this would probably have been no new phenomenon.

Almost incessant fogs envelop the coasts of Monterey Bay, rendering the approach somewhat difficult. Except for

---

[5] September was too early for the gray whale migration. These were most likely humpback whales, possibly blue whales.

this circumstance there would scarcely be a safer shore. No concealed rock extends farther than a cable length from shore, and if the fog is too thick, it is easy to anchor and wait for its clearing up. Then the Spanish settlement is seen in the angle formed by the southern and eastern shores.

The sea was covered with pelicans. It appears that these birds never fly more than five or six leagues from the land, and navigators who encounter them during a fog may be certain of being no further distant from it. We saw them for the first time in Monterey Bay, and I have since been informed that they are common over the whole coast of California. The Spaniards call them *alcatraz*.

A lieutenant colonel, who resides at Monterey, is governor of both Californias.[6] His jurisdiction is more than eight

---

[6] The lieutenant colonel was Pedro Fages, and this was the second time that he had served as governor.

Born in Catalonia in 1730, he had accompanied Portolá and Junipero Serra on the "Sacred Expedition" of 1769 that established the Spanish presence at San Diego and Monterey and discovered San Francisco Bay. Left behind by Portolá at Monterey, Fages built the first presidio and served as Alta California's first governor. A man of great vigor, even restlessness, he undertook the exploration of the Salinas and Santa Clara valleys and left behind a book-length manuscript of his memoirs, *A Historical, Political, and Natural Description of California*. He and Serra quarrelled continually over the respective rights of the soldiers and missionaries, the punishment of Indians, the establishment of new missions, and just about everything else. Serra, himself only five feet three inches tall, described Fages as "a ridiculous little fellow," while Fages complained that Serra conducted himself with "great despotic spirit and total indifference." In 1773 Serra journeyed to Mexico hundred leagues in circumference, but his real subjects consist only of two hundred and eighty-two mounted soldiers, who form the garrison of five small forts[7] and furnish detachments of four or five men to each of the twenty-five missions or parishes into which Old and New California are divided. These slender means are sufficient to secure the obedience of about fifty thousand wandering Indians in this extensive part of America, who continually change their residence, following the season of fishing or hunting. Nearly ten thousand have embraced Christianity.

City specifically to request the removal of Fages, and he succeeded.

Fages was reassigned to Mexico's Sonoran frontier, where he fought with the Apache and with the Yuma of the Colorado River area. He was promoted to lieutenant colonel and in 1782 returned to Monterey, now as governor of both Alta and Baja California. He brought with him his new wife, Doña Eulalia, whose utter misery at Monterey led her to outlandish and desperate acts. She would lock herself in her room, loudly and publicly accuse Fages of adultery, demand divorce, then repent and confess that she had invented the accusations. Her tortured behavior provided the lonely outpost with gossip for a couple of years, before she finally settled down to the role of an obedient, if unhappy, military wife. As for Junipero Serra, nearing the end of his life and having fought even more ferociously with Fages' two successors, Fernando Rivera y Moncada and Felipe de Neve, he was much less critical of Fages in his second term and seemed almost glad to have him back.

Pedro Fages continued as governor about five years after La Pérouse's visit. He retired to Mexico City in 1791, where he died three years later.

[7] The five forts, or *presidios*, were at Loreto in Baja California, and at San Diego, Santa Barbara, Monterey, and San Francisco in Alta California.

These Indians are in general diminutive and weak,[8] and exhibit none of that love of independence and liberty which characterize the nations of the north,[9] of whom they possess neither the arts nor the industry. Their color nearly approaches that of the Negroes whose hair is not woolly. The hair of the Californians is very strong, and would grow to a considerable length, but they cut it off at about four or five inches from the root.[10]

---

[8] The few explorers who saw this area before the establishment of the mission had a better opinion of the Indians. Vizcaíno, for example, characterized them as "a gentle and peaceable people, docile, generous, and friendly, of good stature, fair complexion, and the women possessed of pleasing countenance."

[9] While referring specifically to the natives of Alaska, La Pérouse is validating what was then a generally held opinion that climate made northerners more vigorous, artistic, and morally superior to southerners throughout the world. Montesquieu, for example, wrote in 1748 that people in warmer climates possess "no curiosity, no enterprise, no generosity of sentiment; the inclinations are all passive; indolence constitutes the utmost happiness; scarcely any punishment is so severe as mental employment; and slavery is more supportable than the force and vigor necessary for human conduct." Southerners were also held to be immoral, more prone to criminal behavior, and less able to control the passions. It is interesting to note, then, that much of the criticism that La Pérouse and other early travelers heaped on California Indians was already in place and well articulated before the Indians themselves were encountered.

[10] King Louis XVI, in his instructions to La Pérouse, specifically requested that notes be taken regarding people's hair, nails, and the color and texture of their skin (observing, in particular, changes of color or texture on different parts of the body).

Many of them have beards, while others, according to the missionaries, have never had any. Whether they are naturally bearded is a question which is not even decided in the country itself. The governor, who had been a great traveler into the interior of the land and for fifteen years had resided among these savages, assured us that those who appeared without beards had plucked them out with bivalve shells, which they use as tweezers. The president of the missions,[11] who has resided nearly the same time in California, maintained the contrary opinion. It must be difficult for a stranger to decide between them, but as the governor had traveled over a much greater extent of country than the missionary, his opinion would have predominated with me if I had been forced to decide the question. Obliged, however, to relate precisely what we have seen, we are under the necessity of admitting that we observed beards on only about half the adults; and of these some were of so respectable an appearance that they might have claimed distinction in Turkey or in the vicinity of Moscow.

These Indians are extremely skillful with the bow and killed before us the smallest birds. Their patience in approaching them is inexpressible. They conceal themselves

---

[11] Junipero Serra had died about two years before. The newly-appointed president of the missions was Fermín Francisco Lasuén, who had been serving in California since 1773.

and slide in a manner after their game, seldom shooting until within fifteen paces.

Their industry in hunting larger animals is still more admirable. We saw an Indian with a stag's head fastened on his own, walking on all fours and pretending to graze. He played this pantomime with such fidelity, that our hunters, when within thirty paces, would have fired at him if they had not

been forewarned. In this manner they approach a herd of deer within a short distance, and kill them with their arrows.

■ ▣ ▣ ▣ ▣

Loreto is the only presidio of Old California on the eastern coast of that peninsula. The garrison consists of fifty-four horsemen, who afford small detachments to the fifteen missions [of Old California], the duties of which are performed by Dominicans, who have succeeded the Jesuits and Franciscans.[12] . . . About four thousand Indians, converted and assembled in these fifteen parishes, are the whole fruit of the long apostleship of the different religious orders, who have succeeded each other in this painful ministry. . . .

Northern California, notwithstanding its great distance from Mexico, appears to me to unite infinitely more advantages for the forming of missions than Old California. Its first establishment, which is San Diego, dates only to the 26th of July, 1769. It is the presidio farthest to the south,

---

[12] The Jesuits founded the first Baja California mission in the late 1690s, and continued to expand and support the Baja missions until 1767, when King Carlos III ordered all Jesuits expelled from the Western hemisphere. (The expulsion was the result not of missionary activities, but of a fear in the European courts that the Jesuits were plotting to overthrow the various monarchies there.) The Franciscans then took over management of the missions for a brief time, but in 1773, over-extended because of their expansion into Alta California, they readily agreed to turn the Baja missions over to the Dominicans.

as San Francisco is farthest to the north. This last was built the 9th of October, 1776; that of the channel of Santa Barbara in September, 1786; and Monterey, at present the capital and chief place of the two Californias, on the 3d of June, 1770.

The harbor of this presidio was discovered in 1603 by Sebastián Vizcaíno,[13] commander of a small armed squadron based at Acapulco, by order of Viscount de Monterey,[14] viceroy of Mexico. Since that time the galleons, on their return from Manila, have sometimes come into this bay to procure refreshment after their long passage, but it was not

---

[13] Sebastián Vizcaíno had explored Monterey Bay in 1603. With three ships and two hundred men under his command, he edged along the coast, looking for the fabled Straits of Anias [the Northwest Passage] and also for a safe harbor that might shelter the Manila galleons after their ocean crossing. Although Juan Cabrillo had sailed past Monterey Bay in 1542, it was Vizcaíno who drew excellent maps of the area and bestowed names on its most prominent features. He named Carmel River after the three Carmelite monks who accompanied his ships, named the entire bay after the viscount who sponsored the expedition, and called the northern point of the bay Punta Año Nuevo because it was rounded shortly after New Year's day, 1604. His praise of this excellent (*famoso*) harbor lived in Spanish memory and archives for over a century-and-a-half, eventually drawing the "Sacred Expedition" of Portolá and Serra to Monterey Bay in 1769. Vizcaíno's ancient maps were even then the most up-to-date and reliable that the Spanish government had to give to Portolá.

[14] The office of viceroy was established in 1535, when Don Antonio de Mendoza was sent to Mexico as the embodiment of the Spanish king, thereby curbing the power of Cortes and the conquistadors and pre

until 1770 that the Franciscans established their first mission here.[15] They have ten at present, in which they reckon 5,143 Indians converted. The four following columns will show the name of the parish, the date of the establishment, the presidio on which each parish depends, and the number of converts. The Spaniards give the name of *presidio* generally to all their forts in Africa as well as in America, that are situated in infidel countries; the term implies that there are no colonists but simply a garrison residing in the citadel.[16]

---

serving the authority of the monarch in the New World. [The word *viceroy* means literally "in the place of the king."]

Gaspar de Zuniga y Acebedo, Count of Monterey, arrived in Vera Cruz in 1595. The ninth viceroy, he was said to have been a person of good judgment, not very severe, and generous with royal money. During his tenure Spanish rule was extended and peace brought to many regions of Mexico.

[15] At the time of La Pérouse's visit, the Manila galleons had been sailing between the Philippines (then a Spanish colony) and Acapulco since 1566—more than two hundred years—and they would continue to do so until the Spanish lost Mexico in 1822. These large boats carried some six hundred passengers and were laden with tea, porcelain, spices, silks, and other luxury goods from the Orient. The Manila galleons plied one of the most long-lived and profitable trade routes the world has ever seen. Because the trip from Manila to Acapulco took six to seven months, the Spaniards wanted a port along the California coast where the ships could put in for fresh water and repairs, and where they might find protection from English pirates. Although a presidio was late in coming, the plans for such a port were important in the early explorations of the California coast.

[16] *Presidio*, meaning a military post, derives from the Latin, *praesidere*, to guard or, literally, to sit in front of.

Names of parishes	Names of presidios on which they depend	Date of their establishment	Number of individuals converted
San Carlos	Monterey	June 3, 1770	711
San Antonio	"	July 14, 1771	850
San Luis Obispo	"	Sept. 1, 1772	492
Santa Clara	San Francisco	Jan. 18, 1777	475
San Francisco	"	Oct. 9, 1776	250
San Buenaventura	Santa Barbara	May 3, 1782	120
Santa Barbara	"	Sept. 3, 1786	. . .
San Gabriel	"	Sept. 8, 1771	843
San Juan Capistrano	San Diego	Nov. 1, 1776	544
San Diego	"	July 26, 1769	858
			5143

The piety of the Spaniards has hitherto maintained these missions and presidios at a great expense, with the sole view of converting and civilizing the Indians, a system much more worthy of praise than that of those avaricious individuals who appeared to be invested with national authority for no other purpose than to commit with impunity the most atrocious barbarities. The reader will soon perceive, however, that a new branch of commerce may procure to the Spanish nation greater advantages than the richest mine of Mexico, and that the healthfulness of the air, the fertility of the soil, and the abundance of every kind of fur, for which China is a certain market, afford to this part of America incalculable advantages over Old California. There, the unhealthiness and sterility can never be compensated for by a few pearls, which must be industriously sought at the bottom of the sea.

Before the arrival of the Spaniards, the Indians of California cultivated nothing but a small quantity of maize, and subsisted almost entirely by fishing and hunting.[17] No country is more abundant in fish and game of every description. Hares, rabbits, and deer are extremely common; seals and otters as abundant as in the more northern parts; and in the winter they kill a great number of bears, foxes, wolves, and wild cats.[18]

---

[17] The Indians of the Monterey Bay area did not do any farming before the coming of the Spaniards. In fact, the only California Indians to cultivate maize were those who lived along the Colorado River. Since Pedro Fages had visited that area, we might imagine the source of La Pérouse's misunderstanding. Also, while fishing and hunting were certainly important to the natives of Monterey, the gathering of wild seeds, nuts, and bulbs probably formed the mainstay of their diet.

[18] Hares and rabbits are respectively the black-tailed hare or jackrabbit (*Lepus californicus*) and the brush rabbit (*Sylvilagus bachmani*). The deer is the black-tailed deer (*Odocoileus hemionus columbianus*). The "seals" present in the Monterey Bay area at the time included the California sea lion (*Zalophus californianus*), the Stellar sea lion (*Eumetopias jubata*), the Guadalupe fur seal (*Arctocephalus townsendi*), the northern elephant seal (*Mirounga angustirostris*), and the harbor seal (*Phoca vitulina*). The otter is the sea otter (*Enhydra lutris*). The bear is the California grizzly bear (*Ursus californicus*), which had

The coppices and plains are covered with small grey crested partridges, which live in society like those of Europe but in coveys of three or four hundred.[19] They are fat and of excellent taste.

The trees are inhabited by the most charming birds. Our ornithologist stuffed several varieties of sparrows, blue jays, titmice, speckled woodpeckers, and troupiales.[20] Among the birds of prey, we observed the white-headed eagle, the large

---

always been common in the area [Vizcaíno spotted several of them along the shore feeding on the carcass of a beached whale], but had begun to increase greatly in number with the arrival of Spanish cattle. Foxes are the gray fox (*Urocyon cinereoargenteus*). Wolves (*Canis lupus*), now extinct in California, were once common in the Monterey Bay area, and like the grizzly bear preyed upon the Spanish cattle. Wild cats almost certainly refer to the mountain lion (*Felis concolor*) or the bobcat (*Lynx rufus*), still resident in the mountains near Monterey Bay, although there are historic accounts that suggest jaguars (*Felis onca*) may also have been present at this time.

[19] The California quail (*Callipepla californica*).

[20] Several species of sparrows and related birds are found in the Monterey Bay area in late September. We may assume from this list and from descriptions of the landscape elsewhere in the text that the collecting of "charming birds" that inhabit the trees took place almost entirely in the oak woodland near the coast. In that case, blue jays would have more likely referred to the scrub jay (*Aphelocoma coerulescens*) than the Steller's jay (*Cyanocitta stelleri*). The plain titmouse (*Parus inornatus*) is likewise a resident of the oak woodlands. The spotted woodpecker may be the red-shafted flicker (*Colaptes auratus*), or perhaps Nuttall's woodpecker (*Picoides nuttallii*). The "troupiales" are certainly the dramatically colored northern oriole (*Icterus galbula*).

and small falcon, the goshawk, the sparrow hawk, the black vulture, the large owl, and the raven.[21]

In the ponds and on the seacoast are found the duck, the

---

[21] The white-headed eagle is, of course, the bald eagle (*Haliaeetus leucocephalus*). The large falcon is perhaps a peregrine falcon *(Falco peregrinus)*, the small falcon is most likely the American kestrel or sparrow hawk (*Falco sparverius*). The goshawk is most likely the red-tailed hawk (*Buteo jamaicensis*), a common resident of the area. The sparrow hawk is probably what we call the sharp-shinned hawk (*Accipeter striatus*), very common in the fall, rather than the American kestrel which is the most likely candidate for the "small falcon." The black vulture is the turkey vulture (*Cathartes aura*), and the large owl is the great-horned owl (*Bubo virginianus*). Ravens (*Corvus corax*) are currently rare around the fringes of the bay. Either they have changed their habits in the last two centuries, or La Pérouse might have been referring to the crow (*Corvus brachyrhynchos*).

grey and white pelican with yellow tufts, different species of gulls, cormorants, curlews, ring plovers, small water hens, and herons.[22] Lastly, we killed and stuffed a bee-eater, which ornithologists have supposed to be peculiar to the old continent.[23]

The soil likewise is inexpressibly fertile. Every kind of garden plant thrives astonishingly. We enriched the gardens of the governor and the missions with different grains that we had brought from Paris, which were in perfect preservation, and will add to the sum of their domestic enjoyments.

The crops of maize, barley, wheat, and peas can only be compared to those of Chile. Our European cultivators can form no conception of so abundant a fertility. The medium produce of wheat is seventy or eighty for one and the

---

[22] Mallards (*Anas platyrhynchos*), northern pintails (*A. acuta*), cinnamon teals (*A. cyanoptera*), and northern shovelers (*A. clypeata*) are among the ducks most common this time of year. The brown pelican (*Pelecanus occidentalis*), which La Pérouse calls the grey and white pelican, as well as several species of gulls and cormorants are still present along the coast. The word "curlews" (the French is *courlis*) may have included several species of sandpipers as well as what we call the long-billed curlew (*Numenius americanus*). The ring plovers could be one of several plovers, or perhaps the killdeer (*Charadrius vociferus*). Small water hens are surely the American coots (*Fulica americana*), while among the most spectacular of the herons are the great blue heron (*Ardea herodias*), the great egret (*Casmerodius albus*), and the snowy egret (*Egretta thula*).

[23] The "bee-eater," which was reproduced by an artist with La Pérouse in one of the few illustrations that survived the voyage, is the California thrasher (*Toxostoma redivivum*).

extremes sixty and a hundred.[24] Fruit trees are still very scarce, but the climate is extremely proper for their cultivation and differs little from the southern provinces of France. The cold is never more intense, while the heats of summer are much more moderate on account of the fogs that prevail in these countries and communicate a degree of humidity very favorable to vegetation.

The forest trees are the stone pine, the cypress, the evergreen oak, and the occidental plane tree.[25] They stand apart from each other without underwood, and a verdant carpet, over which it is pleasant to walk, covers the ground.

---

[24] That is, for every bushel of wheat seeds planted, an average of seventy or eighty bushels could be produced. The numbers seem high. In 1792 George Vancouver visited Mission Santa Clara, a location more congenial to wheat growing than Carmel, and he estimated that the proportion there was about twenty-five or thirty to one.

[25] The use of the phrase "stone pine" (le pin á pignon) suggests a pine with an edible nut, which would make one suspect the digger pine (Pinus sabiniana) or perhaps the Coulter pine (P. coulteri). These both grow further inland, however, at least in present times. Pedro Fages has left a description of the Indians setting fire to the bases of pine trees near Mission Carmel to fell the trees and harvest the pine nuts. "The cones of the pine tree are small, and the nuts are extremely so, but very good and pleasing to the taste," he wrote. So perhaps it is the Monterey pine (P. radiata) or the knobcone pine (P. attenuata) that is being described, since both digger pines and Coulter pines have large cones and nuts.

The cypress is surely the Monterey cypress (Cupressus macrocarpa), the evergreen oak is the coast live oak (Quercus agrifola), and the plane tree is the sycamore (Plantanus racemosa).

There are clearings several leagues in extent, forming vast plains that abound in all sorts of game.[26]

The land, though very productive, is sandy and light, and owes its fertility, I believe, to the humidity of the air, for it is badly watered. The nearest running stream to the presidio is two leagues distant. It is a brook that flows near the mission of San Carlos and is called by the ancient navigators Rio de Carmel. This distance was too great to allow us to fetch our water from thence, so we procured it from ponds behind the fort, where it was of a very indifferent quality, scarcely dissolving soap. The Carmel River, which affords

---

[26] Many early travelers commented on the openness of the forests, especially the oak forests. The trees were large and fully formed, the ground beneath them free of underbrush. One early explorer compared such forests to the well-tended "parks" of England.

Forests without understory and clearings without brush are hardly a natural condition. The landscape of the early Monterey Bay area, it is generally thought, was in fact the creation of the Indians who had been burning the land for hundreds of years before the coming of the Spaniards. They burned the land consciously and on a regular basis, using fire to create an environment that was prolific in game animals and rich in edible and other highly desirable plants. Rivera y Moncada, the second governor of Alta California, wrote from Monterey in 1774 that he was having great difficulty in breaking the Indians of their "bad habits." "Having harvested their seeds, they set fires so that new grasses and herbs will come up; also to catch rabbits which get confused by the smoke." Almost everywhere in California the practice of burning the land persisted, and was so necessary to the Indian way of life that among the first laws passed by Europeans wherever they settled were ones that forbade the setting of fires on meadows and in forests.

a wholesome and agreeable drink to the missionaries and their Indians, might also with a little trouble water their gardens.

■ ■ ■ ■ ■

It is with the most pleasing satisfaction that I speak of the pious and prudent conduct of these religious men, which so perfectly agrees with the goal of their institution. I shall not conceal what I conceived to be reprehensible in their internal administration, but I must affirm that, by being individually good and humane, they temper by their mildness and charity the austerity of the rules which have been pre-scribed by their superiors. A friend to the rights of men rather than to theology, I could have wished, I confess, that there had been joined to the principles of Christianity a legislation which might gradually have made citizens of men whose state at present scarcely differs from that of the Negro inhabitants of our colonies, at least in those plantations which are governed with most mildness and humanity.

I am perfectly aware of the extreme difficulty of this new plan. I know that these people have very few ideas, and still less stability, and that if they were to cease to be treated as children, they would escape from those who have taken the pains to instruct them. I know likewise that reasoning can produce very little effect upon them, that it is absolutely necessary to appeal to their senses, and that corporal punishment, with rewards in a double proportion, have hitherto been the only means adopted by their legislators. But would it not be possible for ardent zeal and extreme patience to demonstrate to a few families the advantages of society founded on the rights of the people; to establish among them the possession of property, so bewitching to all men; and by this new order of things to engage everyone to cultivate his field by emulation, or to direct his exertions to some other employment?

I admit that the progress of this new civilization would be very slow, and the attentions necessary to be paid extremely tedious; that the theater of action is very remote, and that the applause of the enlightened part of mankind would never reach the ear of him who should thus have consecrated his life to deserve them. Neither do I hesitate to affirm that human motives are insufficient for such a ministry, and that the enthusiasm of religion, with the rewards it promises, can alone compensate for the sacrifices, the boredom, the fatigue, and the dangers of this kind of life. Still I could wish that the minds of the austere, charitable, and religious individuals I have met with in these missions were a little more tinctured with the spirit of philosophy.

I have already expressed my true opinion regarding the monks of Chile, whose irregularity appeared to me in general to be scandalous. There are monks of merit in Chile, but in general they enjoy a degree of liberty contrary to the state they have embraced.[27] With the same freedom I shall portray these truly apostolic men who have abandoned the indolent life of a cloister to deliver themselves up to fatigue and cares of every kind. According to my custom, I shall proceed with our own history while I relate theirs, and place before the eyes of the reader what we saw and learned during our short stay at Monterey.

---

[27] About eight months previously, La Pérouse had rounded Cape Horn and put in at the Bay of Concepción, Chile. He describes the monks there, living in a colonial town of some 10,000 inhabitants, as being "the worst subjects in America. . . .

"Their effrontery is inexpressible. I have seen them stay at a ball till midnight, remote indeed from the better company, mixing with the servants. No one gave more accurate information to the younger part of my crew than these monks regarding places of which priests ought to have had no knowledge, except for the purpose of putting others upon their guard."

2

We anchored on the 14th of September in the evening, two leagues from the shore, in sight of the presidio and of two vessels which were in the roadstead. They had fired guns every quarter of an hour to direct us to the anchorage, which they thought might be concealed by the fog. At ten in the evening, the captain of the corvette *la Favorita* came on board in his longboat and offered to pilot our vessels into the port. The corvette *la Princesa*[1] had likewise sent a pilot on board the Astrolabe.

---

[1] A *corvette* was a three-masted warship with a single deck and ship rigging. It was smaller than a *frigate*, whose three masts were square-rigged and which had two decks.

La Princesa, a vessel of some 189 tons, was built at San Blas in 1777 and 1778. It was designed with enough storage space so that it could

We learned that these two vessels were Spanish, commanded by Don Estevan Martínez, lieutenant of a frigate from the department of San Blas in the province of Guadalajara. The government maintains a small marine force in that port,[2] subject to the orders of the viceroy of Mexico. It consists of four corvettes of twelve guns, and a schooner, the particular destination of which is the supply of the presidios of northern California with provisions. These are the same vessels which made the last two expeditions of the Spaniards on the northwest coast of America,[3] and they are

---

sail for over a year without having to restock. Built for durability rather than speed, it served for over three decades. *La Favorita*, somewhat larger (it displaced 193 tons), was built in Peru and purchased for the San Blas fleet in 1777. Both ships were heavily used. Fairly well armed with cannons, they took part in many explorations as well as in the work-a-day task of provisioning the California missions.

[2] San Blas, in what is now the state of Nayarit, was established in 1768 as a supply center for the new California colonies. It had a shipyard, a naval center, and warehouses where goods were assembled.

[3] Worried by the rumored Russian expansion into Alaska, Spain launched those expeditions to the northwest coast during the 1770s. Those referred to by La Pérouse were most likely the 1775 expedition of Bruno de Hezeta and Juan Francisco de la Bodega y Quadra, and the 1779 expedition of Ignacio de Arteaga and (again) Bodega y Quadra.

The 1775 expedition, despite losing several men because of an Indian attack, ultimately reached Vancouver Island and southern Alaska. The two ships were the *Santiago*, the largest boat ever built at San Blas, and the *Sonora*, a two-masted schooner only thirty-six feet in length and twelve feet in beam. It was on this expedition that Trinidad Bay in northern California was explored, and Bodega Bay just north of San

sometimes sent as packet boats to Manila for the more speedy transmission of the orders of the court.

At ten in the morning we weighed, and anchored in the roadstead at noon. We were saluted with seven guns, which we returned, and I sent an officer to the governor with the letter of the Spanish minister, which had been forwarded to me in France before my departure. It was not sealed and was addressed to the viceroy of Mexico, whose authority extends to Monterey, though at the distance of eleven hundred leagues by land from the capital.

Mr. Fages, commandant of the fort of the two Californias, had already received orders to afford us the same reception as the vessels of his own nation. He executed these orders with a degree of earnestness and benevolence which deserve our warmest acknowledgements. He did not confine himself to mere verbal politeness. Cattle, garden vegetables, and milk were sent on board in abundance. The desire of serving us seemed even to disturb the harmony between the commander of the two vessels and the chief of the fort. Each was desirous of exclusively providing for our wants; and when the account was to be discharged we were obliged to insist

---

Francisco was entered and named. The 1779 expedition consisted of *La Princesa* and *La Favorita*. It reached as far north as Prince of Wales Sound and Cook's Inlet. On both expeditions diaries were kept, maps made, and rituals performed to take possession of the land in the name of Spain.

on their receiving our money. The vegetables, milk, poultry, and the assistance of the garrison in wooding and watering were afforded *gratis*; the cattle, sheep, and corn were charged at so low a price that it was evident a bill had been presented to us merely because we had insisted upon it.[4] To these generous proceedings of Mr. Fages the utmost politeness was added. His house was our home, and all his people were at our disposal.

The fathers of the mission of San Carlos, at the distance of two leagues from Monterey, soon arrived at the presidio.[5] No less obliging than the officers of the two vessels and the fort, they invited us to dine with them and promised to inform us minutely concerning the government of their missions, the manner of living of the Indians, their arts, their newly acquired habits, and in general everything that could rouse the curiosity of travelers. We eagerly accepted this invitation, which we should not have failed to solicit if we had not thus been anticipated. It was agreed that we should set out in two days. Mr. Fages wanted to accompany us and undertook to procure horses.

---

[4] Almost every early traveler to California would comment upon the extraordinary generosity of the people here—the legendary "Spanish hospitality."

[5] Fermín Lasuén, president of the California mission, and Matías Noriega were then serving at Carmel Mission.

After crossing a small plain covered with herds of cattle[6] and in which there were only a few trees, which were necessary to shelter these animals against the rain and the sun, we ascended the hills. From there we heard the sound of bells announcing our arrival, of which the missionaries had been previously informed by a horseman from the governor.

We were received like the lords of manors when they first take possession of their estates. The president of the missions, in his ceremonial vestments and with his holy water sprinkle in his hand, awaited us at the gate of the church, which was illuminated in the same manner as on the greatest feast days. He conducted us to the foot of the high altar, where he chanted the *Te Deum* in thanksgiving for the happy outcome of our voyage.

Before we entered the church, we had passed through a square in which the Indians of both sexes were ranged in a line. They exhibited no marks of surprise in their countenance, and left us in doubt whether we should be the subject of their conversation for the rest of the day.

---

[6] Cattle prospered when introduced to California. In the 1770s milk saved the mission and presidio from starvation when crops repeatedly failed —although it has been suggested that an inability to digest milk might have brought on some of the illnesses that swept through the Indian community. In later years cattle hides and tallow would be the mainstay of the *rancho* economy, so much so that hides would be popularly known as "California banknotes."

The church is neat though thatched with straw. It is dedicated to Saint Charles,[7] and adorned with some tolerable pictures, copied from originals in Italy. Among them is a picture of hell, in which the painter appears to have borrowed from the imagination of Callot;[8] but as it is absolutely necessary to strike the imagination of these new converts with the most lively impressions, I am persuaded that such a representation was never more useful in any country. It would be impossible for the protestant worship, which proscribes images and almost all the ceremonies of our church, to make any progress with this people. I doubt whether the picture of paradise, which sits opposite that of hell, produces so good an effect upon them. The state of tranquility which it represents, and that mild satisfaction of the elect who surround the throne of the Supreme Being, are ideas too sublime

---

[7] Two men named Carlos—Carlos III, King of Spain, and Carlos de Croix, viceroy of Mexico—determined that this mission be named after San Carlos (Saint Charles) Borromeo. Saint Charles was an Italian saint of the sixteenth century. Born into the Medici family, he was a priest at twelve and a cardinal at twenty-two. He played an important role at the Council of Trent, and worked to enforce its reforms.

[8] Jacques Callot was a seventeenth century French engraver. Credited with being the first European artist to depict the horrors of war, he was especially known for his portrayal of the macabre. In his *Temptations of Saint Anthony*, for example, the hermit's cavern is filled with hellish throngs of skeletons, demons with bat wings, seductive women with long claws, etc.

for the minds of uncultivated savages. But it was necessary to place rewards by the side of punishment, and it was a point of duty that no change should be permitted in the kind of enjoyments which the Catholic religion promises to man.

On coming out of the church we passed through the same row of Indians, whom the *Te Deum* had not induced to abandon their post. Only the children had removed to a small distance and formed groups near the house of missionaries, which, along with the different storehouses, is opposite the church. The Indian village stands on the right, consisting of about fifty huts which serve for seven hundred and forty persons of both sexes, including their children,

who compose the mission of San Carlos, or of Monterey.

These huts are the most wretched anywhere. They are round and about six feet in diameter and four in height.[9] Some stakes, the thickness of a man's arm, stuck in the ground and meeting at the top, compose the framing. Eight or ten bundles of straw, ill arranged over these stakes, are the only defense against the rain or wind; and when the weather is fine, more than half the hut remains uncovered, with the precaution of two or three bundles of straw to each habitation to be used as circumstances may require.

This general architecture of the two Californias has never undergone the smallest change, notwithstanding the exhortations of the missionaries. The Indians say that they love the open air, that it is convenient to set fire to their house

---

[9] If fifty "huts" (cabanes in French) indeed served 740 people, it would mean an average of about fifteen people per dwelling—obviously ridiculous for a structure six feet in diameter and four feet high. Even if we assume that most of the women were locked up at night in the dormitorio, this would still suggest a level of overcrowding that is physically impossible.

Perhaps part of the explanation lies in the season. Despite the fog, September tends to be the warmest month in the Monterey Bay area, and people may have been sleeping outside, using the tule structures more for storage than as true dwellings. It is also quite possible that the missionaries, hoping to convince the Indians of the virtues of living like Europeans, did not give them time, materials, or encouragement to maintain proper native-style dwellings; the "huts" which La Pérouse describes might have been left over from the previous winter, which would explain their run-down condition.

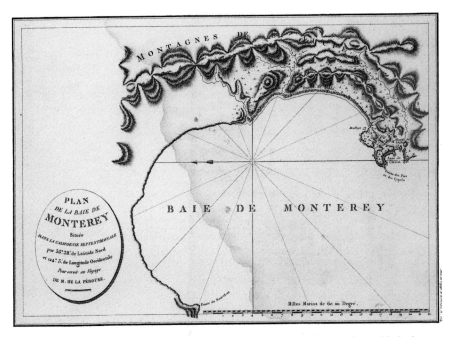

Map of Monterey Bay from Voyage de La Pérouse autour du Monde, *published in 1797. This and all subsequent plates are reproduced courtesy of the Bancroft Library, University of California, Berkeley, unless otherwise noted.*

View of Monterey, 1792. Sketch by John Sykes, master's mate aboard Vancouver's ship, Discovery, *that visited Monterey in 1792 and again in 1794.*

John Sykes.

19

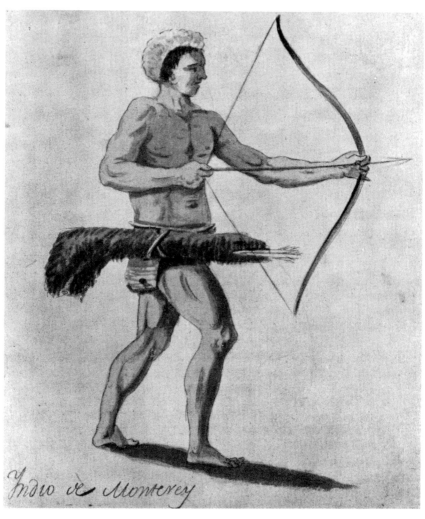

Indian of Monterey, 1791. Sketch probably by José Cardero, one of the two artists attached to the Spanish expedition led by Alejandro Malaspina that visited Monterey in mid-September, 1791.

Indian woman of Monterey, 1791, by José Cardero. The woman is wearing a rabbit-skin cape and a tule skirt with a deer-skin coverlet. Photo courtesy of Smithsonian Institution.

Indians of Monterey, 1791, by José Cardero.

The California Indian Way of Fighting (Modo de Pelear de los Indios de California), *1791, by José Cardero.*

Mission Carmel, 1791, by José Cardero. Note that five years after La Pérouse's visit the buildings were still low with thatched roofs and the "courtyard" barren. A cluster of Indian houses is barely visible in the background.

25

Monterey

View of the "convent," church, and Indian village of Mission Carmel, 1791, by José Cardero.

View of the presidio, 1791, by José Cardero. An unfinished sketch in which one can make out an Indian ramada (shade house) in the foreground, corrals for animals, ox carts, and (to the left) what appear to be water tanks .

Plaza of the presidio, 1791, by José Cardero.

The reception of La Pérouse at Mission Carmel, 1786. A copy of an original painting done by Duché de Vancy, an artist with La Pérouse. Courtesy of Bancroft Library, Berkeley.

Portrait of "Giovanni Francesco di Lapérouse"
by an Italian engraver, reproduced in the
California Historical Society Quarterly,
Volume 20, 1941.

Brown thrasher and a pair of
California quail, as drawn by Prevost
Junior, botanical illustrator with the
La Pérouse expedition.

when the fleas become troublesome, and that they can build another in less than two hours. The independent tribes, who as hunters so frequently change their residence, have of course an additional motive.[10]

The color of these Indians, which is that of Negroes; the house of the missionaries; their storehouses, which are built of brick and plastered; the appearance of the ground on which the grain is trodden out; the cattle, the horses—everything in short—brought to our recollection a plantation at Santo Domingo or any other West Indian island. The men and women are collected by the sound of a bell; a missionary leads them to work, to the church, and to all their exercises. We observed with concern that the resemblance is so perfect that we have seen both men and women in irons, and others in the stocks. Lastly, the noise of the whip might have struck our ears, this punishment also being administered, though with little severity.

The monks answering our different questions left us ignorant of no part of the government of this religious community, for no other name can be given to the administration they have established. They are the temporal as well

---

[10] The dwellings that La Pérouse describes, made of tule rather than straw, were indeed better adapted to the migratory habits of the Indians than to a permanent settlement. Nevertheless, when the Indians at Carmel were finally forced into European-style houses several years later, terrible epidemics broke out and devastated the Indian community.

as the spiritual governors, the products of the earth being entrusted to their care. The day consists in general of seven hours labor and two hours prayer, but there are four or five hours of prayer on Sundays and feast days, which are entirely consecrated to rest and divine worship.

Corporal punishment is inflicted on the Indians of both sexes who neglect the exercises of piety, and many sins, which in Europe are left to Divine justice, are here punished by irons and the stocks. And lastly, to complete the similarity between this and other religious communities, it must be observed that the moment an Indian is baptized, the effect is the same as if he had pronounced a vow for life. If he escapes to reside with his relations in the independent villages, he is summoned three times to return; if he refuses, the missionaries apply to the governor, who sends soldiers to seize him in the midst of his family and conduct him to the mission, where he is condemned to receive a certain number of lashes with the whip. As these people are at war with their neighbors, they can never escape to a distance greater than twenty or thirty leagues. They have so little courage that they never make any resistance to the three or four soldiers who so evidently violate the rights of men in their persons. This custom, against which reason so strongly exclaims, is kept up because theologians have decided that they could not in conscience administer baptism to men so inconstant unless the government would in some measure serve as their sponsor and answer for their perseverance in the faith.

The predecessor of Mr. Fages, Mr. Filipe de Neve,[11] commander of the interior provinces of Mexico, a man replete with humanity and a Christian philosopher who died about four years ago, remonstrated against the practice. He

---

[11] Filipe de Neve was governor of California, headquartered at Monterey between 1777 and 1782. As with his predecessors, Pedro Fages and Fernando Rivera y Moncada, de Neve found himself in a prolonged and bitter conflict with Junipero Serra. De Neve attempted to train Indians for self-government by having the Indians of each mission elect officers who would be outside the control of the missionaries. Serra opposed and ultimately sabotaged the effort. De Neve, on his part, resisted Serra's demands that runaways be pursued back to their native villages, fought against expanding the number of missions, and was responsible for establishing the *pueblos* of San José and Los Angeles, hoping to create a civilian base that would moderate the power of both the missionaries and the military. Especially infuriating to Serra, de Neve disputed the mission president's right to confirm Indians. These two powerful men, one at the presidio, the other at the mission a few miles away, isolated from the rest of the world, clearly hated each other. De Neve at various times called Serra "arrogant," "obstinate," "willfully deceitful," and an "artful contriver." Serra complained in a letter to Lasuén that he could scarcely bear de Neve's presence. "It is worse even than my physical suffering. Today [I celebrated mass] with much difficulty. The nights I pass without much sleep; but the reason for this may not be so much my legs as the chief at the presidio."
In 1782 de Neve was promoted to inspector-general of the frontier region that included California, Texas, and parts of northern Mexico. He died shortly thereafter, in 1784.

thought that the progress of the faith would be more rapid and the prayers of the Indians more agreeable to the Supreme Being if they were not constrained. He desired a constitution less monastic, affording more civil liberty to the Indians and less despotism in the executive power of the presidios, the government of which might fall into the hands of cruel and avaricious men. He thought likewise that it might perhaps be necessary to moderate their authority by the appointment of a magistrate who might be the tribune, as it were, of the Indians, and possess sufficient authority to defend them from harassments. This upright man had borne arms in service of his country from his infancy, but he was exempt from the prejudices of his profession, and well knew that military government is subject to great improprieties when not moderated by an intermediate power. He might, however, have experienced the difficulty of maintaining the conflict of three authorities in a country so remote from the governor-general of Mexico, since the missionaries, though pious and respectable, are already at open variance with the governor, who appears to me to be a worthy military character.

▣ ▣ ▣ ▣ ▣

We were desirous of being present at the distributions made at each meal, and as all the days with this kind of religious community were exactly alike, by recording the proceedings of one, the reader will be acquainted with the history of a whole year.

The Indians as well as the missionaries rise with the sun, and immediately go to prayers and mass, which last for an hour. During this time three large boilers are set on the fire for cooking a kind of soup, made of barley meal, the grain of which has been roasted previous to its being ground. This sort of food, of which the Indians are extremely fond, is called *atole*.[12] They eat it without either butter or salt, and it would certainly to us be a most insipid mess.

Each hut sends for the allowance of all its inhabitants in a vessel made of the bark of a tree.[13] There is neither confusion nor disorder in the distribution, and when the boilers are nearly emptied, the thicker portion at the bottom is distributed to those children who have said their catechism the best.

The time of repast is three quarters of an hour, after which they all go to work, some to till the ground with oxen, some to dig in the garden, while others are employed in domestic occupations, all under the eye of one or two missionaries.

---

[12] The word is not native to California, but is Nahuatl (Aztec), and was adopted and brought north by the Spaniards.

[13] No such container has ever been reported from this area, nor are there even trees whose bark would lend itself to the purpose. One assumes that La Pérouse was observing the water-tight baskets of the Indians, but did not look too closely at them.

The women have no other employment than their household affairs, the care of their children, and the roasting and grinding of corn. This last operation is both tedious and laborious, because they have no other method of breaking the grain than with a roller upon a stone.[14] Mr. de Langle, who saw this operation, made a present of his mill to the missionaries. It was difficult to have rendered them a greater service, since four women will now do the work of a hundred,

[14] It seems that a *mano* and *metate* are being described, rather than the native mortar and pestle.

thus leaving them time to spin the wool of their sheep and manufacture some coarse cloths.[15]

But the missionaries have hitherto been more attentive to their heavenly than their earthly concerns, and have greatly neglected the introduction of the most common arts. They are so austere as to their own comforts that they have no fireplace in their chambers, though the winter is sometimes severe. The greatest anchorites have never lived a more edifying life. Father Fermín de Lasuén, president of the missions of New California, is one of the most worthy and respectable men I have ever met. His mildness, charity, and affection for the Indians are beyond expression.

At noon the bells give notice of the time of dinner. The Indians then quit their work, and send for their allowance in the same vessel as at breakfast. But this second soup is thicker than the former, and contains a mixture of wheat, maize, peas, and beans; the Indians call it *pozole*.[16]

They return to work from two to four or five o'clock, when they repair to evening prayer, which lasts nearly an hour and is followed by a distribution of *atole*, the same as

---

[15] George Vancouver, who visited Mission Carmel in 1792, made no comment on the use of the mill, and noted instead that the only method of grinding corn was with the *mano* and *metate*. Nor is there evidence that de Langle's gift was used in later years.

[16] Pozole is a Nahuatl (Aztec) word.

at breakfast. These three distributions are sufficient for the subsistence of the greater number of these Indians, and we might perhaps adopt this economical food in years of scarcity, with the addition of some seasoning.

The whole art of this cookery consists in roasting the grain before it is reduced to meal. As the Indian women have no clay or metallic vessels for this operation, they perform it in baskets of bark by using small burning wood coals.[17] They turn these vessels with such dexterity and rapidity that they succeed in causing the grain to swell and burst without burning the basket, though made of combustible material. (We can affirm that our best coffee is far from being roasted with equal skill.) It is distributed to them every morning, and the slightest embezzlement is punished by the whip, though it seldom happens that they expose themselves to the danger.

These punishments are adjudged by Indian magistrates, called *caciques*.[18] There are three in each mission, chosen by

---

[17] The coals are bounced in the basket with the grain.

[18] Two of the *caciques* were Athanasia and Carlos Juan, as they were known in Spanish, both Rumsen men originally from the village of Tucutnut, a couple of miles upstream from the mission on the banks of the Carmel River.

Cacique is an Arawak word for chief, taken from the Caribbean and carried by the Spaniards throughout the New World. These *caciques* or "magistrates," were probably the *alcaldes* (chiefs) and *regidores* the people from among those whom the missionaries have not excluded. However, to give a proper notion of this magistracy, we must observe that these *caciques* are like the overseers of a plantation: passive beings, blind performers of the will of their superiors. Their principal functions consist in serving as beadles in the church, to maintain order and the appearance of attention.

Women are never whipped in public, but in an enclosed and somewhat distant place that their cries may not excite a too lively compassion, which might cause the men to revolt. The latter, on the contrary, are exposed to the view of all their fellow citizens, that their punishment may serve as an example. They usually ask pardon for their fault, in which case the executioner diminishes the force of his lashes, but the number is always irrevocable.

The rewards are small distributions of grain, of which they make little thin cakes, and bake them on hot wood ashes. On high festivals an allowance of beef is distributed which many eat raw, particularly the fat, considered by them as delicious as the finest butter or the most excellent cheese. They skin all animals with the greatest dexterity, and when

---

(counselors) elected by the Indians in accordance with de Neve's laws. Although these officials were supposedly independent, Serra and the other Franciscans refused to grant them any real power, claiming that the Indians were not yet ready for self-government.

an animal is fat they make, like the ravens, a croaking of pleasure, devouring with their eyes those parts for which they have the greatest desire.

The Indian men are often permitted to hunt and fish for

their own benefit, and upon their return they generally make a present to the missionaries of a part of their fish or game. But they proportion the quantity to what is strictly necessary for their consumption, taking care to increase it when they know that their superiors have any visitors or guests.

The women raise some poultry about their huts, the eggs of which they give to their children. These fowls are the property of the Indians, as are their clothes, small articles of furniture, and implements of hunting.

There is no example of theft among them, though the door of their hut consists merely of a bundle of straw, which they place across the entrance when the inhabitants are absent. These manners may appear patriarchal to some of our readers, who may not reflect that in these huts there is no article which can excite the avarice of a neighboring hut. The food of the Indians is secured to them, and they have therefore no other want than that of giving life to beings who are sure to be as simple as themselves.

The men in these missions have made greater sacrifices to Christianity than the women, because, before its introduction, they were accustomed to polygamy, and were even in the habit of espousing all the sisters of the same family. The women, on the contrary, have acquired the right of receiving exclusively the caresses of a single man.

I must confess, however, notwithstanding the unanimous report of the missionaries concerning this pretended polygamy, that I am at a loss to conceive how it could have been established in a nation of savages; with the number of men being nearly equal to that of the women, the consequence must have been a forced continence in many individuals, unless conjugal fidelity were less rigorously observed than in the missions, where the holy fathers have constituted themselves guardians of the virtue of the women.[19] An hour after supper, they take care to secure all the women whose husbands are absent, as well as the young girls above the age of nine years, by locking them up, and during the day they entrust them to the care of elderly women. All these precautions are still inadequate, and we have seen men in the stocks and women in irons for having eluded the vigilance

---

[19] Although polygamy was practiced, in general it was only chiefs or the wealthiest men who had more than one wife.

of these female Arguses, whose eyes are not sufficient for the complete performance of their office.

The converted Indians have preserved all the ancient customs which their new religion does not prohibit. They have the same huts, the same games, and the same clothes. The clothing of the richest consists of a garment of otter skin, which descends from the waist somewhat lower than the groin. The most indolent have simply a piece of cloth, which the mission supplies, to conceal nudity, and a small cloak of rabbit skin, tied under the chin, which covers their shoulders, and descends to their waist. The rest of their body is absolutely naked, as is their head. Some of them, however, have straw hats, which are neatly made.

The clothing of the women is a mantle of deer skin, badly tanned. Those of the missions have generally a small corset with sleeves, which, with a small apron of rushes and a petticoat of deerskin descending to the middle of the leg and covering their loins, is the whole of their dress. Young girls more than nine years of age have simply a cloth around their waist, and the children of both sexes are entirely naked.

The hair both of men and women is cut to the length of about four or five inches. The Indians of the *rancherias*,[20]

---

[20] *Rancheria* means an Indian village or settlement; the term is still used to describe some of the smaller Indian reservations in California.

having no instruments of iron, perform this operation with lighted fire-brands. They are likewise in the habit of painting their bodies red in general, and when they are in mourning, in black. The missionaries have forbidden the first of these paintings, but they are obliged to tolerate the other because these people are so strongly attached to their friends. When they are called to their remembrance they shed tears, though they may have lost them for a considerable period; and if their name be mentioned by anyone, even through inadvertence, they consider it an offense.

The bonds of relationship have less force with them than those of friendship. Children take scarcely any notice of their father. They abandon his hut as soon as they are capable of providing for their subsistence. But they preserve a longer attachment for their mother, who has brought them up with extreme mildness and has never beaten them except when they have shown cowardice in their combats with children of the same age.

The old men of the *rancherias,* who are no longer able to hunt, are supported at the expense of their whole village, and are in general well respected. The independent savages are frequently at war, but the fear of the Spaniards causes them to respect the missions, and this perhaps is not the smallest of the inducements which increase the Christian villages. Their weapons are the bow and arrow, which is armed with a flint[21] very skillfully made. The bows, which are wood and strung with the tendon of an ox, are very superior to those of the inhabitants of *Port des Français.*[22]

We were assured that they neither eat their prisoners nor their enemies slain in war. Nevertheless, when they have vanquished and killed the chiefs or bravest men on the field of battle, they devour some small portions, less in token of hatred or vengeance than as homage due to their valor. They believe that this food is calculated to increase their courage. Like the Canadians, they scalp the vanquished, and take out their eyes, which they have the art of preserving from corruption, and which they carefully keep as tokens of victory.[23] They burn their dead and deposit their ashes in cemeteries.

---

[21] Arrowheads were made of chert, found locally, or of obsidian which came to the area by trade.

[22] Port des Français, or "Frenchmen's Harbor," is an inlet in Alaska, just south of Cape Fairweather, discovered by La Pérouse shortly before his arrival in Monterey. It is now called by its Indian name Lituya Bay.

[23] Scalping may have been practiced. It has been reported from elsewhere in California, and there is evidence that it might have predated the coming of Europeans. La Pérouse must have heard of ritual cannibalism from Pedro Fages, who also mentions it in his memoirs. There have been, as far as I know, no other reports of this custom from California, and indeed such a practice would seem to contradict the fastidiousness, fear, and respect with which California Indians treated the dead. As for the "art" of eyeball preservation, one strongly suspects that La Pérouse is repeating a "horror" story that the monks or soldiers were circulating among themselves.

They have two kinds of games, in which they employ their whole leisure. The first, to which they give the name of *takersia*, consists of throwing a small hoop of three inches in diameter causing it to roll in a space of twenty feet square, cleared of grass and surrounded with stakes. The two players each hold a stick of the thickness of a common cane and five feet long. This stick they endeavour to strike through the small hoop while it is in motion. If they succeed, they gain two points, and if the hoop should stop so as to lie upon the stick, they reckon but one. The game is three points. The diversion affords an energetic degree of exercise, because the hoop or the stick is always in action.

The other game, named *toussi,* is more tranquil. It is played by four persons, two on each side. Each in turn conceals in one of his hands a piece of wood, while his partner makes a thousand gestures to occupy the attention of the

adversaries. It is curious enough to a bystander to see them squatted down opposite each other, keeping the most profound silence, observing the traits of the countenance and the most minute circumstances, which may assist their guessing the hand which conceals the piece of wood. They gain or lose a point accordingly as their guess is right or wrong, and those who gain it have a right to hide in their turn. The game is five points, the usual stake glass beads, and with the independent Indians, the favors of their women.[24]

These Indians have no knowledge of a God or of a future state, with the exception of some nations to the south, who had a confused notion of this kind before the arrival of the missionaries. Those of the south placed their paradise in the middle of the sea, where the elect were to enjoy cool breezes, which never prevail on their burning sands; and they supposed hell to be in the cavities of their mountains.

The missionaries, persuaded from their prejudices and perhaps from their experience that the reason of these men is scarcely ever developed, consider this a just motive for treating them like children, and admit only a very small number to the communion. These are the geniuses of the country, who, like Descartes and Newton, would have enlightened their age and countrymen by teaching them that four

---

[24] *Takersia,* the hoop and stick game, was widespread in California and apparently of ancient origin. It is thought to predate the introduction of the bow and arrow, about 500 A.D., when hunters depended primarily on spears.

The game described as *toussi* is obviously the one variously called "grass game," "hand game," or "peon," and still played today, although generally with more players on a team and always with considerable singing rather than silence.

and four make eight, which is a calculation beyond the reach of a great number of them.

The plan pursued by these missionaries is little calculated to remove this state of ignorance, in which everything is directed to the recompenses of another life, while the most usual arts, even the surgery of our villages, are not exercised. Many children perish in consequence of hernias, which the slightest skill would cure, and our surgeons had the pleasure of relieving a small number, and of showing them how to apply the necessary bandages.

It must be confessed that if the Jesuits were neither more pious nor more charitable than these missionaries, they were at least more intelligent and skillful. The immense edifice which they have raised at Paraguay cannot fail to excite admiration,[25] but their ambition and prejudices have afforded matter for the strongest reproach, in their system of community of property, so contrary to the progress of civilization and imitated with too much servility in the missions of California.

This government is a true theocracy for the Indians, who believe that their superiors have immediate and continual communication with God, and that they cause him to descend

---

[25] The "Jesuit Empire" in South America was known throughout the world. It consisted of about thirty mission villages, eight of which were in modern-day Paraguay. By the end of the seventeenth century the population of these villages exceeded 100,000, and the mission lands and buildings were said to be valued at $28,000,000.

every day on the altar. By virtue of this opinion, the holy fathers live in the midst of the villages with the greatest security. Their doors are not shut, even in the night, though the history of their mission affords the example of a missionary slain. It is known that this assassination was the consequence of a commotion occasioned by an act of imprudence, for homicide is a very rare crime, even among the independent Indians.[26] It is, however, not otherwise revenged, except by general contempt; but if a man fall beneath the blows of a considerable number of people, it is concluded that he deserved his fate, since his conduct produced such a number of enemies.

---

[26] La Pérouse seems to be combining two separate incidents into a single story. Father Luís Jayme was killed in an Indian revolt at Mission San Diego in 1775. Serra, while clearly distraught at the event, saw it as part of the Divine plan. "Thank God!" he said. "The blood of a martyr has fertilized the soil, and the conversion of the gentiles is assured."

The revolt at Mission San Diego seems to have been a general uprising, however, caused by no particular incident but rather by overall conditions. The "act of imprudence" suggests the attempted murder that took place at Mission San Gabriel a few years before. An Indian chief attacked a soldier who had raped his wife. The soldier survived. The chief was killed and his head cut off and impaled on a pole as a warning to others.

3

Northern California, of which the most northerly settlement is that of San Francisco, in latitude 37° 58', has no other boundary, according to the opinion of the governor of Monterey, than that of America, and our vessels, by penetrating as far as Mount St. Elias in Alaska, did not reach its limits.

To the motives of piety, which have led Spain to sacrifice large sums for the support of its presidios and missions, there are at present considerable reasons of state to be added, which may direct the attention of government to this valuable part of America. Here sea otter skins are as common as in the Aleutian Islands and those of the other seas frequented by the Russians.

We found at Monterey a Spanish commissary, Mr. Vicente Vasadre y Vega, who had brought orders to the governor enjoining him to collect all the sea otter skins of his four presidios and the ten missions, all of which the government reserves to itself the exclusive commerce.[1] Mr. Fages assured me that twenty thousand might be collected annually. As he was well acquainted with the country, he added that if the China trade could furnish a demand for thirty thousand skins, two or three settlements to the north of San Francisco would soon procure them for the commerce of his nation.

---

[1] In 1784 published accounts of James Cook's voyages confirmed rumors that had already been circulating throughout Europe. Sea otter fur had become the height of fashion among the Mandarin Chinese—so much so that a single skin, which could be purchased for almost nothing from natives along the Pacific coast of North America, would fetch as much as $80 to $120 in China. In response to these reports Vicente Vasadre y Vega proposed to the Spanish authorities an ambitious trade venture. He would arrange to purchase sea otter skins from California and send them to Canton by way of Manila. At Canton they would be traded for jars of Chinese quicksilver, which miners in the New World needed to help separate gold from its ore. Not only would this produce wealth, but it would head off the other trading nations who were already launching expeditions to Alaskan waters. The Spanish viceroy, Bernardo de Gálvez, agreed to generously finance the Vasadre y Vega scheme.

In the months following La Pérouse's visit, Vasadre y Vega collected skins from Carmel and the other missions and presidios. He then set out for Canton. Although he found the market glutted when he arrived —French and English merchantmen had already beaten him to the punch—he nevertheless signed a reasonable contract with the Chinese. The sea otter trade between Spain and China, however, lasted only a

It is perfectly unaccountable that the Spaniards, having so near and so frequent intercourse with China from Manila, should have been hitherto ignorant of the value of this precious trade of furs.

It is to Captain Cook, and the publication of his work that they are indebted for this dawn of information, which will procure them the greatest advantages. This great man has thus traveled for the benefit of all nations, and his own country derives no greater advantage above others except the glory of the enterprise and of reckoning him among her sons.

The sea otter is an amphibious animal as common along the whole west coast of America, from the 28th to the 60th degree of north latitude, as the seal on the coast of Labrador and in Hudson's Bay. The Indians are by no means so expert seamen as the Eskimos. The boats at Monterey are only made of reeds. The inhabitants of the missions of Santa Barbara and San Diego have wooden canoes, constructed nearly in the same manner as those of the inhabitants of

---

few more years. In California it caused disruptions: Indians neglected their mission duties and soldiers stole from the Indians when this new source of income appeared. In Manila the trading companies, jealous of their exclusive privileges, were hostile. Finally, the Spanish government, while insisting on its right to maintain a monopoly, was unwilling to pay adequately or on time for the skins it purchased. By the mid-1790s the sea otter trade officially collapsed, although foreign ships would enter California waters illegally to engage in a contraband trade that lasted throughout the rest of the Spanish colonial period.

Maui, but without outriggers. The Indians of Monterey catch the sea otter either on shore with snares, or kill them with large sticks when they find them at a distance from the sea. For this purpose they conceal themselves behind the rocks, this animal being frightened at the least noise and plunging immediately into the water.[2] Before the present year, the skin of an otter bore no higher value than two hare skins. The Spaniards, never suspecting there could be any demand for them, had not sent any to Europe, and Mexico was too hot a country for them to suppose that this article could be acceptable there.

I am of the opinion that in a few years a great revolution will take place in the commerce of the Russians at Kiatcha[3] from the difficulty of supporting this competition. From the comparison I have made of the sea otter skins of Monterey with those of Port des Français, I am inclined to believe that the skins of the south are rather inferior, but the difference is so small that I am not absolutely certain of this inferiority and I doubt whether it may make a difference of ten per cent

---

[2] Sea otters today almost never venture on land, their habits having changed drastically after the massive fur hunts of the early nineteenth century nearly drove them to extinction.

[3] La Pérouse is referring to the town of Kiakhta or Kiachta, just south of Lake Baikal on the Siberian-Chinese border. It was a major stop on the caravan route by which Russians exchanged furs, lambskins, cloth, and linen for Chinese goods such as tea, silks, nankeen cloth, and porcelains.

in the sale. It is almost certain that the new company of Manila will endeavour to seize this branch of trade; this would be the most fortunate event which could happen to the Russians, because it is the nature of exclusive privileges to annihilate or at least to paralyze all the branches of commerce and industry, while perfect freedom alone can communicate to both all the activity of which they are susceptible.

◘ ◘ ◘ ◘ ◘

New California, notwithstanding its fertility, does not yet possess a single European colonist.[4] A few soldiers who have married Indian women and either live in the forts or are scattered in small parties on public service and the different missions, constitute at present the whole of the Spanish nation in this part of America. If it were closer to Europe, it would be in no respect inferior to Virginia, which lies in the same latitude. But its proximity to Asia may well compensate for this, and I am convinced that good laws, particularly freedom of trade, would soon procure it a certain number of inhabitants. Such reforms are necessary, since the possessions of Spain are so extensive that it is impossible to suppose the population can rise for a long time to come

---

[4] It is curious that La Pérouse did not know or failed to mention anything about the *pueblos* established at San José and Los Angeles.

in any of her colonies. The great number of individuals of both sexes who, from religious principle, have devoted themselves to celibacy, and the invariable policy of the government to admit but one religion and to employ the most violent means for supporting it, must constantly impose a new obstacle to every augmentation.

The government of the villages converted to Christianity would be more favorable to increased population if property and a certain degree of liberty constituted its basis. Nevertheless, since the establishment of ten different missions of Northern California, the fathers have baptised 7,701 Indians of both sexes, and buried only 2,388. But it must be remarked that this computation does not, like those of our European towns, inform us whether the population increases or diminishes, because they are continually baptizing independent Indians. It merely shows that Christianity extends itself, and I have already observed that the affairs of the next world cannot be placed in better hands.

■ ■ ■ ■ ■

The Franciscan missionaries are almost all Europeans. They have a college, for so they call a convent in Mexico, of which the general of his order in America is the guardian. This house does not depend upon the provincial head of the Franciscans of Mexico, but has its superiors in Europe.[5]

The viceroy is at present the sole judge of every dispute between the different missions, which do not acknowledge the authority of the commandant at Monterey. This officer is merely obliged to supply them with military force when they demand it, but as he has a power over all the Indians, particularly those of the *rancherias,* and moreover has the command of all the detachments of cavalry which reside in the missions, these different relations very frequently disturb the harmony between the military and the religious government. But the latter possesses sufficient influence in the mother country in all cases to prevail. These affairs were formerly brought before the governor of the inland provinces, but the new viceroy, Don Bernardo Galvez, has united all the powers in his own person.[6]

Spain allows annually four hundred pesos to each mis-

---

[5] San Fernando College was established by the Franciscans in Mexico City in 1733. It housed over a hundred friars, and was often the first stop for European missionaries on their way to California. It also served as a retirement home for those who completed their missionary work. The daily routine included being awakened at midnight for two hours of chanting, and then being awakened again at 5 a.m. for a full day of chanting meditations, matins, masses, lauds, litanies, and vespers. There were also courses in the Indian languages of Mexico, the methods of organizing and maintaining a mission, and theology.

[6] Bernardo de Gálvez had become the forty-ninth viceroy, taking over from his father, Matías de Gálvez. The father was an old man of great

sionary, whose number is fixed at two for a parish, and if there is a supernumerary, he receives no salary. Money is of very little use in a country where nothing can be purchased. Beads are the only money of the Indians. The college of Mexico therefore never sends a single dollar in cash, but the value in effects, such as tapers for the church, chocolate, sugar, oil, wine, and some pieces of cloth, which the missionaries divide into small girdles to cover what decency does not permit the converted Indians to expose.

The governor's pay is four thousand pesos; that of his deputy four hundred and fifty; and that of the captain inspector of two hundred and eighty-three horsemen, distributed through the two Californias, two thousand. Each horseman receives two hundred and seventeen, but out of this he is obliged to provide his subsistence and to furnish himself with a horse, clothing, arms, and all sorts of necessities in general. The government, which has stud horses and herds

---

integrity, known as a protector of the arts. The son, although young, had had wide military experience. He had fought in the Apache wars on the northern borderlands of Mexico and had led a successful and highly praised campaign against the British in the Mississippi Valley during the American Revolution. Characterized as ambitious, affable, and popular with the Mexican people, he fell under official suspicion when it was rumored that his rebuilding the Castle of Chapultepec in Mexico City was a prelude to the secession of New Spain from the monarchy. Bernardo de Gálvez served as viceroy for only about a year, dying, despite his youth and vigor, in 1786 after a brief illness.

of cattle, sells horses to the soldiers, as well as meat for their consumption. The price of a good horse is eight pesos, and that of an ox, five. The governor has the management of the breeding horses and cattle herds, and at the end of the year he gives an account to each horseman of the balance which may be due to him in money, which he pays with the utmost punctuality.

As the military, of whom there were only eighteen at the presidio, had rendered us many little services, I requested permission to present them with a piece of blue cloth;[7] and I sent the missions coverlets, cloth goods, glass, beads, iron tools and implements, and generally all the small effects which might be necessary to them and which we had not had occasion to distribute to the Indians at Port des Français. The president informed the whole village, that it was a present from their faithful and ancient allies, who professed the same religion as the Spaniards. This so particularly excited their benevolence that the day after, each of them brought us a truss of hay or straw for the cattle and sheep we were about to send on board. Our gardener gave the missionaries some Chilean potatoes in perfect preservation, which in my opinion was not the least valuable of our presents,

---

[7] In these days before textile factories, cloth was indeed a generous gift. In Monterey at that time a shirt was valued at three to four times the cost of a calf, more than a bull, or about as much as a horse.

and which will certainly thrive in the light but fertile soil of the environs of Monterey.[8]

From the day of our arrival we were busily employed in supplying ourselves with wood and water, and we were allowed to cut the former as near as possible to the place of our landing. Our botanists did not lose a moment in adding to their collection of plants; but the season was very unfavorable, the heat of the summer having entirely dried them up and their seed being scattered on the ground. Those which Mr. Collignon could distinguish were the common wormwood, sea wormwood, the male southernwood, mugwort, Mexican tea, Canadian goldenrod, the Italian starwort, millefoil, deadly nightshade, spurry and water mint.[9] The gardens of the governor and of the missions were filled with an infinity of

---

[8] Mr. Collignon of the King's Garden had been assigned to the La Pérouse expedition, charged both with collecting exotic and potentially useful plants and introducing new plants for the benefit of native people and far-flung colonies.

The potato was a native of the Andes, cultivated there for some two thousand years. It was introduced into Europe in the sixteenth century. Despite the fact that the expedition had stopped in Chile, it is likely that the Chilean potatoes which Mr. Collignon gave the missionaries had been brought from Europe, since they are listed as part of the ship's cargo when La Pérouse departed from France.

[9] The first four plants mentioned (common wormwood, sea wormwood, southernwood, and mugwort) are all members of the *Artemisia* genus. Perhaps they caught the attention of Collignon because of the uses of such plants in Europe, both as medicine and as the basic ingredient of absinthe. Mexican tea is a member of the *Chenopodium*, or pigweed

plants for culinary use, which were furnished us in such abundance that our people had in no country been better supplied with vegetables.

Our lithologists were equally zealous as our botanists, but they were still less fortunate. They met with nothing on the mountains, in the ravines, or on the shore but a light clayey stone very easily decomposed which is a kind of marl. They found likewise blocks of granite, the veins of which contained crystallized feldspar, some rounded fragments of porphyry and jasper, but they observed no trace of metal.

Shells are not more abundant than stones, with the exception of some superb heliotes [abalones], of which the pearl is of the most beautiful luster. They are nine inches long and four in breadth. The other shells are not worth enumerating. There are small olivellas, whelks, and different sea snails [*tequla* or turban snails], but they are not at all curious. The eastern and southern coasts of old California are much

---

genus, of by-and-large edible plants. The Canadian goldenrod is *Solidago canadensis*. The Italian starwort (*Stellaria sp.*) is a chickweed, also known as an edible green. Millefoil (*Achillea millefolium*) is yarrow, renowned for medicinal properties. The deadly nightshade (*Solanum sp.*) belongs to a family remarkable for producing not only edible plants, but narcotic plants, medicinal plants, and poisonous plants. Spurry probably refers to the sand-spurry (*Spergularia sp.*) rather than the European spurry (*Spergula*); it is related to the chickweed. True mints (*Mentha sp.*) are almost all exotics from Europe. Perhaps *Lycopus americanus*, the water horehound, is being described.

richer in this part of natural history. They afford oysters
containing pearls equal in beauty and magnitude to those
of Ceylon or the Persian Gulf. These would also be an
article of great value and certain sale in China, but it is
impossible for the Spaniards to give activity to all the means
of industry which their country furnishes.

■ ■ ■ ■ ■

On the 22nd of September in the evening everything was
loaded and we took leave of the governor and missionaries.
We carried away with us as large a store of provisions as
when we departed from Concepción, Chile. The whole stock
of poultry of Mr. Fages and the missionaries had been
transferred into our hencoops, and we were supplied with
corn, beans, and peas in such plenty that they had left
themselves scarcely more than was strictly necessary. They
refused for a long time to receive any payment, and yielded
only to our pressing offers in consequence of the representation we made to them that they were the administrators
and not the proprietors of the stores of the missions.

On the 23d the wind was contrary, and in the morning of
the 24th we set sail with a breeze from the west. Don Estevan
Martínez had regularly come on board at daybreak, and his
longboat and crew were constantly at our disposal, and had

rendered us every assistance. Indeed I can but feebly express the gratitude we owe him for this estimable conduct, as well as Mr. Vicente Vasadre y Vega, a young man of talents and merit, who was on the point of repairing to China, to conclude a treaty relative to the trade of otter skins.

Heyday Books publishes books on California history, literature, and Native American life. For a catalog, please write us at P.O. Box 9145, Berkeley, CA 94709. (510) 549-3564. FAX (510) 549-1889.

The Harvest Gypsies: On the Road to the Grapes of Wrath. By John Steinbeck, introduction by Charles Wollenberg. A collection of newspaper reports on migrant farm workers that Steinbeck wrote in 1936, three years before *The Grapes of Wrath*.

Indian Summer: Traditional Life among the Choinumne Indians of California's San Joaquin Valley. By Thomas Jefferson Mayfield, introduction by Malcolm Margolin. The reminiscences of a man who spent his childhood with the Choinumne Yokuts in the 1850s, this is the only account by any outsider who lived among a California Indian people while they were still following their traditional ways.

The Ohlone Way: Indian Life in the San Francisco—Monterey Bay Area. By Malcolm Margolin, illustrations by Michael Harney. This well-loved classic vividly recreates the lost world of the Indian people who lived in the San Francisco Bay area such a short time ago.

No Rooms of Their Own: Women Writers of Early California. By Ida Rae Egli. A collection of writings by fifteen extraordinary women draws a new picture of early California and its true pioneers.

Malcolm Margolin, who wrote the introduction and provided commentary to the text, is author of *The Ohlone Way: Indian Life in the San Francisco-Monterey Bay Area* and publisher of *News from Native California*, a quarterly magazine devoted to California Indian history and culture. In 1995 he received the Fred Cody Award for lifetime achievement from the Bay Area Book Reviewers Association.

Linda Gonsalves Yamane, illustrator, is a freelance artist and cultural historian. She lives in the Monterey Bay area and traces her ancestry to the Rumsien, the native people of Monterey.